Brahmacharya

The Road of Ultimate Knowledge

Swami Vivekananda

Institute of Thought & Philosophy

GRAPEVINE INDIA

Published by

GRAPEVINE INDIA PUBLISHERS PVT LTD

www.grapevineindia.com
Delhi | Mumbai
email: grapevineindiapublishers@gmail.com

Ordering Information:
Quantity sales: Special discounts are available on quantity purchases by corporations, associations, and others.
For details, reach out to the publisher.

First published by Grapevine India 2024

The mission of the Institute of Thought and Philosophy is to preserve and propagate the teachings of Swami Vivekananda. This great Indian spiritual leader is known for introducing the West to Hinduism. Drawing from his vast literary legacy, we provide valuable insights and practical guidance for modern living.

Have any query or feedback? Please reach out to us at
ITPPress123@gmail.com

On Brahmacharya

Brahmacharya should be like a burning fire within the veins!

ब्रह्मचर्यप्रतिष्ठायां वीर्यलाभः ॥३८॥

By the establishment of continence energy is gained. The chaste brain has tremendous energy and gigantic will-power. Without chastity there can be no spiritual strength. Continence gives wonderful control over mankind. The spiritual leaders of men have been very continent, and this is what gave them power. Therefore the Yogi must be continent.

Complete continence gives great intellectual and spiritual power. The Brahmachârin must be sexually pure in thought, word, and deed. Lose regard for the body; get rid of the consciousness of it so far as possible.

Is there a greater strength than that of Brahmacharya—purity, my boy?

Save the spiritual store in your body by observing continence.

Non-killing, truthfulness, non-stealing, continence, and nor-receiving are called Yamas.

A man who wants to be a perfect Yogi must give up the sex idea. The soul has no sex; why should it degrade itself with sex ideas? Later on we shall understand better why these ideas must be given up. The mind of the man who receives gifts is acted on by the mind of the giver, so the receiver is likely to become degenerated. Receiving gifts is prone to destroy the independence of the mind, and make us slavish. Therefore, receive no gifts.

By continence, reverence, and devotion to Guru, success comes after a long time (as in the case of Indra).

प्रणतिब्रह्मचर्यपसर्पणानि कृत्वा सिद्धिबहुकालात्तद्वत् ॥१९॥

That which all the Vedas declare, which is proclaimed by all penances, seeking which men lead lives of continence, I will tell you in one word — it is 'Om'." You will find this word "Om" praised very much in the Vedas, and it is held to be very sacred.

Teach the boys the system of Brahmacharya.

The modern system of education gives no facility for the development of the knowledge of Brahman. We must found Brahmacharya Homes as in times of old.

But now we must lay their foundations on a broad basis, that is to say, we must introduce a good deal of change into it to suit the requirements of the times. Of this I shall speak to you later on.

"That piece of land to the south of the Math, we must also purchase in time. There we shall start an Annasatra — a Feeding Home. There arrangements will be made for serving really indigent people in the spirit of God. The Feeding Home will be named after Shri Ramakrishna. Its scope will at first be determined by the amount of funds. For the matter of that, we may start it with two or three inmates. We must train energetic Brahmacharins to conduct this Home. They will have to collect the funds for its maintenance — ay, even by begging. The Math will not be allowed to give any pecuniary help in this matter. The Brahmacharins themselves shall have to raise funds for it. Only after completing their five years' training in this Home of Service, will they be allowed to join the Temple of Learning branch. After a training of ten years — five in the Feeding Home and five in the Temple of Learning — they will be allowed to enter the life of Sannyasa, having initiation from the Math authorities — provided of course they have a mind to become Sannyasins and the Math authorities consider them fit for Sannyasa and are willing to admit them into it. But the Head of the Math will be free to confer Sannyasa on any exceptionally meritorious Brahmacharin, at any time, in defiance of this rule. The ordinary Brahmacharins, however, will have to qualify themselves for Sannyasa by degrees, as I have just said. I have all these ideas in my brain."

First of all, comes the gift of food; next is the gift of learning, and the highest of all is the gift of knowledge. We must harmonise these three ideals in the Math. By continuously practising the gift of food, the Brahmacharins will have the idea of practical work for the sake of others and that of serving all beings in the spirit of the Lord firmly impressed on their minds. This will gradually purify their minds and lead to the manifestation of Sâttvika (pure and unselfish) ideas. And having this the Brahmacharins will in time acquire the fitness for attaining the knowledge of Brahman and become eligible for Sannyasa.

Simply by the observance of strict Brahmacharya (continence) all learning can be mastered in a very short time — one has an unfailing memory of what one hears or knows but once. It is owing to this want of continence that everything is on the brink of ruin in our country.

You have now to make the character of Mahavira your ideal. See how at the command of Ramachandra he crossed the ocean. He had no care for life or death! He was a perfect master of his senses and wonderfully sagacious. You have now to build your life on this great ideal of personal service. Through that, all other ideals will gradually manifest in life. Obedience to the Guru without questioning, and strict observance of Brahmacharya — this is the secret of success.

As on the one hand Hanumân represent the ideal of service, so on the other hand he represents leonine courage, striking the whole world with awe. He has not the least hesitation in sacrificing his life for the good of Rama. A supreme indifference to everything except the service of Rama, even to the attainment of the status of Brahmâ and Shiva, the great World-Gods! Only the carrying out of Shri Rama's behest is the one vow of this life! Such whole-hearted devotion is wanted. Playing on the Khol and Kartâl and dancing in the frenzy of Kirtana has degenerated the whole people. They are, in the first place, a race of dyspeptics — and if in addition to this they dance and jump in that way, how can they bear the strain? In trying to imitate the highest Sâdhana, the preliminary qualification for which is absolute purity, they have been swallowed in dire Tamas. In every district and village you may visit, you will find only the sound of the Khol and Kartâl! Are not drums made in the country? Are not trumpets and kettle-drums available in India? Make the boys hear the deep-toned sound of these instruments. Hearing from boyhood the sound of these effeminate forms of music and listening to the kirtana, the country is well-nigh converted into a country of women. What more degradation can you expect? Even the poet's imagination fails to draw this picture! The Damaru (An hour-glass-shaped drum, held in Shiva's hand.) and horn have to be sounded, drums are to be beaten so as to raise the deep and martial notes, and with "Mahavira, Mahavira" on your lips and shouting "Hara, Hara, Vyom, Vyom" , the quarters are to be reverberated. The music which awakens only the softer feelings of man is to be stopped now for some time. Stopping the light tunes such as Kheâl and Tappâ for some time, the people are to be accustomed to hear the Dhrupad music. Through the thunder-roll of the dignified Vedic hymns, life is to be brought back into the country. In everything the austere spirit of heroic manhood is to be revived. In following such an ideal lies the good of the people and the country. If you can build your character after such an ideal, then a thousand others will follow. But take care that you do not swerve an inch from the ideal. Never lose heart. In eating, dressing, or lying, in singing or playing, in enjoyment or disease, always manifest the highest moral courage. Then only will you attain the grace of Mahâshakti, the Divine Mother.

Social Conference Address

It seems God created the Brâhmin, God created the Kshatriya, but who created the Sannyasin?

There have been and are Sannyasins or monks in every known religion. There are Hindu monks, Buddhist monks, Christian monks, and even Islam had to yield its rigorous denial and take in whole orders of mendicant monks.

There are the wholly shaved, the partly shaved, the long hair, short hair, matted hair, and various other hirsute types.

There are the sky-clad, the rag-clad, the ochre-clad, the yellow-clad (monks), the black-clad Christian and the blue-clad Mussulman. Then there have been those that tortured their flesh in various ways, and others who believed in keeping their bodies well and healthy. There was also, in odd days in every country, the monk militant. The same spirit and similar manifestations haste run in parallel lines with the women, too — the nuns. Mr. Ranade is not only the President of the Indian Social Conference but a chivalrous gentleman also: the nuns of the Shrutis and Smritis seem to have been to his entire satisfaction. The ancient celibate Brahmavâdinis, who travelled from court to court challenging great philosophers, do not seem to him to thwart the central plan of the Creator — the propagation of species; nor did they seem to have lacked in the variety and completeness of human experience, in Mr. Ranade's opinion, as the stronger sex following the same line of conduct seem to have done.

We therefore dismiss the ancient nuns and their modern spiritual descendants as having passed muster.

The arch-offender, man alone, has to bear the brunt of Mr. Ranade's criticism, and let us see whether he survives it or not.

It seems to be the consensus of opinion amongst savants that this world-wide monastic institution had its first inception in this curious land of ours, which appears to stand so much in need of "social reform".

The married teacher and the celibate are both as old as the Vedas. Whether the Soma-sipping married Rishi with his "all-rounded" experience was the first in order of appearance, or the lack-human-experience celibate Rishi was the primeval form, is hard to decide just now. Possibly Mr. Ranade will solve the problem for us independently of the hearsay of the so-called Western Sanskrit scholars; till then the question stands a riddle like the hen and egg problem of yore.

But whatever be the order of genesis, the celibate teachers of the Shrutis and Smritis stand on an entirely different platform from the married ones, which is perfect chastity, Brahmacharya.

If the performance of Yajnas is the corner-stone of the work-portion of the Vedas, as surely is Brahmacharya the foundation of the knowledge-portion.

Why could not the blood-shedding sacrificers be the exponents of the Upanishads — why?

On the one side was the married Rishi, with his meaningless, bizarre, nay, terrible ceremonials, his misty sense of ethics, to say the least; on the other hand, the celibate monks tapping, in spite of their want of human experience, springs of spirituality and ethics at which the monastic Jinas, the Buddhas, down to Shankara, Ramanuja, Kabir, and Chaitanya, drank deep and acquired energy to propagate their marvellous spiritual and social reforms, and which, reflected third-hand, fourth-hand from the West, is giving our social reformers the power even to criticise the Sannyasins.

At the present day, what support, what pay, do the mendicants receive in India, compared to the pay and privilege of our social reformers? And what work does the social reformer do, compared to the Sannyasin's silent selfless labour of love?

But they have not learnt the modern method of self-advertisement!!

The Hindu drank in with his mother's milk that this life is as nothing — a dream! In this he is at one with the Westerners; but the Westerner sees no further and his conclusion is that of the Chârvâka — to "make hay while the sun shines". "This world being a miserable hole, let us enjoy to the utmost what morsels of pleasure are left to us." To the Hindu, on the other hand, God and soul are the only realities, infinitely more real than this world, and he is therefore ever ready to let this go for the other.

So long as this attitude of the national mind continues, and we pray it will continue for ever, what hope is there in our anglicised compatriots to check the impulse in Indian men and women to renounce all "for the good of the universe and for one's own freedom"?

And that rotten corpse of an argument against the monk — used first by the Protestants in Europe, borrowed by the Bengali reformers, and now embraced by our Bombay brethren — the monk on account of his celibacy must lack the realisation of life "in all its fullness and in all its varied experience!" We hope this time the corpse will go for good into the Arabian Sea, especially in these days of plague, and notwithstanding the filial love one may suppose the foremost clan of Brahmins there may have for ancestors of great perfume, if the Paurânika accounts are of any value in tracing their ancestry.

By the bye, in Europe, between the monks and nuns, they have brought up and educated most of the children, whose parents, though married people, were utterly unwilling to taste of the "varied experiences of life".

Then, of course, every faculty has been given to us by God for some use. Therefore the monk is wrong in not propagating the race — a sinner! Well, so also have been given us the faculties of anger, lust, cruelty, theft, robbery, cheating, etc., every one of these being absolutely necessary for the maintenance of social life, reformed or unreformed. What about these? Ought they also to be maintained at full steam, following the varied-experience theory or not? Of course the social reformers, being in intimate acquaintance with

God Almighty and His purposes, must answer the query in the positive. Are we to follow Vishvâmitra, Atri, and others in their ferocity and the Vasishtha family in particular in their "full and varied experience" with womankind? For the majority of married Rishis are as celebrated for their liberality in begetting children wherever and whenever they could, as for their hymn-singing and Soma-bibbing; or are we to follow the celibate Rishis who upheld Brahmacharya as the sine qua non of spirituality?

Then there are the usual backsliders, who ought to come in for a load of abuse — monks who could not keep up to their ideal — weak, wicked.

But if the ideal is straight and sound, a backsliding monk is head and shoulders above any householder in the land, on the principle, "It is better to have loved and lost."

Compared to the coward that never made the attempt, he is a hero.

If the searchlight of scrutiny were turned on the inner workings of our social reform conclave, angels would have to take note of the percentage of backsliders as between the monk and the householder; and the recording angel is in our own heart.

But then, what about this marvellous experience of standing alone, discarding all help, breasting the storms of life, of working without any sense of recompense, without any sense of putrid duty? Working a whole life, joyful, free — not goaded on to work like slaves by false human love or ambition?

This the monk alone can have. What about religion? Has it to remain or vanish? If it remains, it requires its experts, its soldiers. The monk is the religious expert, having made religion his one métier of life. He is the soldier of God. What religion dies so long as it has a band of devoted monks?

Why are Protestant England and America shaking before the onrush of the Catholic monk?

Vive Ranade and the Social Reformers! — but, O India! Anglicised India! Do not forget, child, that there are in this society problems that neither you nor your Western Guru can yet grasp the meaning of — much less solve!

Chastity

Think of a space in your heart, and in the midst of that space think that a flame is burning. Think of that flame as your own soul and inside the flame is another effulgent light, and that is the Soul of your soul, God. Meditate upon that in the heart.

Chastity, non-injury, forgiving even the greatest enemy, truth, faith in the Lord, these are all different Vrittis. Be not afraid if you are not perfect in all of these; work, they will come.

He who has given up all attachment, all fear, and all anger, he whose whole soul has gone unto the Lord, he who has taken refuge in the Lord, whose heart has become purified, with whatsoever desire he comes to the Lord, He will grant that to him. Therefore worship Him through knowledge, love, or renunciation.

This doctrine of prenatal influence is now slowly being recognized, and science as well as religion calls out: 'Keep yourself holy, and pure.' So deeply has this been recognized in India, that there we even speak of adultery in marriage, except when marriage is consummated in prayer. That is the secret of the race — chastity.

The Hindus, to keep up a high standard of chastity in the race, have sanctioned child-marriage, which in the long run has degraded the race. At the same time, I cannot deny that this child-marriage makes the race more chaste. What would you have? If you want the nation to be more chaste, you weaken men and women physically by child-marriage. On the other hand, are you in England any better off? No, because chastity is the life of a nation. Do you not find in history that the first death-sign of a nation has been unchastity? When that has entered, the end of the race is in sight. Where shall we get a solution of these miseries then? If parents select husbands and wives for their children, then this evil is minimised. The daughters of India are more practical than sentimental. But very little of poetry remains in their lives. Again, if people select their own husbands and wives, that does not seem to bring much happiness. The Indian woman is generally very happy; there are not many cases of quarrelling between husband and wife. On the other hand in the United States, where the greatest liberty obtains, the number of unhappy homes and marriages is large. Unhappiness is here, there, and everywhere. What does it show? That, after all, not much happiness has been gained by all these ideals. We all struggle for happiness and as soon as we get a little happiness on one side, on the other side there comes unhappiness.

. . . In my opinion, a race must first cultivate a great respect for motherhood, through the sanctification and inviolability of marriage, before it can attain to the ideal of perfect chastity. The Roman Catholics and the Hindus, holding marriage sacred and inviolate, have produced great chaste men and women of immense power. To the Arab, marriage is a contract or a forceful possession, to be dissolved at will, and we do not find there the development of the idea of the virgin or the Brahmachârin. Modern Buddhism — having fallen among races who had not yet come up to the evolution of marriage — has made a travesty of monasticism. So until there is developed in Japan a great and sacred ideal about marriage (apart from mutual attraction and love), I do not see how there can be great monks and nuns. As you have come to see that the glory of life is chastity, so my eyes also have been opened to the necessity of this great sanctification for the vast majority, in order that a few lifelong chaste powers may be produced.

The idea is the same everywhere regarding the chastity; of women, whose deviation from it is fraught with danger, but in the case of men it does not matter so much. The Frenchman is, no doubt, a little freer in this respect, and like the rich men of other countries cares not for criticism. Generally speaking, in Europe, the majority of men do not regard a little lax conduct as so very bad, and in the West, the same is the case with bachelors. The parents of young students consider it rather a drawback if the latter fight shy of women, lest they become effeminate. The one excellence which a man must have, in the West, is courage. Their word "virtue" and our word "Viratva" (heroism) are one and the same. Look to the derivation of the word "virtue" and see what they call goodness in man. For women, they hold chastity as the most important virtue, no doubt. One man marrying more than one wife is not so injurious to society as a woman having more than one husband at the same time, for the latter leads to the gradual decay of the race. Therefore, in all countries good care is taken to preserve the chastity of women. Behind this attempt of every society to preserve the chastity of women is seen the hand of nature. The tendency of nature is to multiply the population, and the chastity of women helps that tendency. Therefore, in being more anxious about the purity of women than of men, every society is only assisting nature in the fulfilment of her purpose.

The object of my speaking of these things is to impress upon you the fact that the life of each nation has a moral purpose of its own, and the manners and customs of a nation must be judged from the standpoint of that purpose. The Westerners should be seen through their eyes; to see them through our eyes, and for them to see us with theirs — both these are mistakes. The purpose of our life is quite the opposite of theirs. The Sanskrit name for a student,

Brahmachârin, is synonymous with the Sanskrit word Kâmajit. (One who has full control over his passions.) Our goal of life is Moksha; how can that be ever attained without Brahmacharya or absolute continence? Hence it is imposed upon our boys and youth as an indispensable condition during their studentship. The purpose of life in the West is Bhoga, enjoyment; hence much attention to strict Brahmacharya is not so indispensably necessary with them as it is with us.

The history of the world shows that evil is a continuously increasing quantity, as well as good. Take the lowest man; he lives in the forest. His sense of enjoyment is very small, and so also is his power to suffer.

His misery is entirely on the sense-plane. If he does not get plenty of food, he is miserable; but give him plenty of food and freedom to rove and to hunt, and he is perfectly happy. His happiness consists only in the senses, and so does his misery also.

But if that man increases in knowledge, his happiness will increase, the intellect will open to him, and his sense-enjoyment will evolve into intellectual enjoyment. He will feel pleasure in reading a beautiful poem, and a mathematical problem will be of absorbing interest to him. But, with these, the inner nerves will become more and more susceptible to miseries of mental pain, of which the savage does not think.

Take a very simple illustration. In Tibet there is no marriage, and there is no jealousy, yet we know that marriage is a much higher state. The Tibetans have not known the wonderful enjoyment, the blessing of chastity, the happiness of having a chaste, virtuous wife, or a chaste, virtuous husband. These people cannot feel that.

And similarly they do not feel the intense jealousy of the chaste wife or husband, or the misery caused by unfaithfulness on either side, with all the heart-burnings and sorrows which believers in chastity experience. On one side, the latter gain happiness, but on the other, they suffer misery too.

Twelve years of absolute truthfulness in thought, word, and deed gives a man what he wills. Be chaste in thought, word, and action. Chastity is the basis of all religions. Personal purity is imperative.

Purity

If we are pure, we cannot see impurity. It may exist, but not for us. See only God in every man, woman and child; see it by the antarjyotis , "inner light", and seeing that, we can see naught else.

All religion is to be based upon morality, and personal purity is to be counted superior to Dharma. In this connection it ought to be known that Âchâra means purity inside and outside. External purity can be attained by cleansing the body with water and other things which are recommended in the Shâstras. The internal man is to be purified by not speaking falsehood, by not drinking, by not doing immoral acts, and by doing good to others. If you do not commit any sin, if you do not tell lies, if you do not drink, gamble, or commit theft, it is good. But that is only your duty and you cannot be applauded for it. Some service to others is also to be done. As you do good to yourself, so you must do good to others.

As says our great philosopher Kapila, if purity has not been the nature of the soul, it can never attain purity afterwards, for anything that was not perfect by nature, even if it attained to perfection, that perfection would go away again. If impurity is the nature of man, then man will have to remain impure, even though he may be pure for five minutes. The time will come when this purity will wash out, pass away, and the old natural impurity will have its sway once more. Therefore, say all our philosophers, good is our nature, perfection is our nature, not imperfection, not impurity — and we should remember that. Remember the beautiful example of the great sage who, when he was dying, asked his mind to remember all his mighty deeds and all his mighty thoughts. There you do not find that he was teaching his mind to remember all his weaknesses and all his follies. Follies there are, weakness there must be, but remember your real nature always — that is the only way to cure the weakness, that is the only way to cure the follies.

"Blessed are the pure in heart, for they shall see God." This sentence alone would save mankind if all books and prophets were lost. This purity of heart will bring the vision of God. It is the theme of the whole music of this universe. In purity is no bondage. Remove the veils of ignorance by purity, then we manifest ourselves as we really are and know that we were never in bondage. The seeing of many is the great sin of all the world. See all as Self and love all; let all idea of separateness go. . . .

External purity is very easy and all the world rushes towards [it]. If a certain kind of dress is the kind of morality [to be observed], any fool can do that. When it is grappling with the mind itself, it is hard work.

The people who do external, superficial things are so self-righteous! I remember, when I was a boy, I had great regard for the character of Jesus Christ. [Then I read about the wedding feast in the Bible.] I closed the book and said, "He ate meat and drank wine! He cannot be a good man."

We are always losing sight of the real meaning of things. The little eating and dress! Every fool can see that. Who sees that which is beyond? It is culture of the heart that we want. ... One mass of people in India we see bathing twenty times a day sometimes, making themselves very pure. And they do not touch anyone. ... The coarse facts, the external things! [If by bathing one could be pure,] fish are the purest beings.

Bathing, and dress, and food regulation — all these have their proper value when they are complementary to the spiritual. .... That first, and these all help. But without it, no amount of eating grass... is any good at all. They are helps if properly understood. But improperly understood, they are derogatory. ...

This is the reason why I am explaining these things: First, because in all religions everything degenerates upon being practiced by [the ignorant]. The camphor in the bottle evaporated, and they are fighting over the bottle.

Another thing: ... [Spirituality] evaporates when they say, "This is right, and that is wrong." All quarrels are [with forms and creeds] never in the spirit. The Buddhist offered for years glorious preaching; gradually, this spirituality evaporated. ... [Similarly with Christianity.] And then began the quarrel whether it is three gods in one or one in three, when nobody wants to go to God Himself and know what He is. We have to go to God Himself to know whether He is three in one or one in three.

It is in love that religion exists and not in ceremony, in the pure and sincere love in the heart. Unless a man is pure in body and mind, his coming into a temple and worshipping Shiva is useless. The prayers of those that are pure in mind and body will be answered by Shiva, and those that are impure and yet try to teach religion to others will fail in the end. External worship is only a symbol of internal worship; but internal worship and purity are the real things. Without them, external worship would be of no avail. Therefore you must all try to remember this.

The Light Divine within is obscured in most people. It is like a lamp in a cask of iron, no gleam of light can shine through. Gradually, by purity and unselfishness we can make the obscuring medium less and less dense, until at last it becomes as transparent as glass. Shri Ramakrishna was like the iron cask transformed into a glass cask through which can be seen the inner light as it is. We are all on the way to become the cask of glass and even higher and higher reflections. As long as there is a "cask" at all, we must think through material means. No impatient one can ever succeed.

I should very much like our women to have your intellectuality, but not if it must be at the cost of purity. I admire you for all that you know, but I dislike the way that you cover what is bad with roses and call it good. Intellectuality is not the highest good. Morality and spirituality are the things for which we strive. Our women are not so learned, but they are more pure. To all women every man save her husband should be as her son. To all men every woman save his own wife should be as his mother. When I look about me and see what you call gallantry, my soul is filled with disgust. Not until you learn to ignore the question of sex and to meet on a ground of common humanity will your women really develop. Until then they are playthings, nothing more. All this is the cause of divorce. Your men bow low and offer a chair, but in another breath they offer compliments. They say, 'Oh, madam, how beautiful are your eyes!' What right have they to do this? How dare a man venture so far, and how can you women permit it? Such things develop the less noble side of humanity. They do not tend to nobler ideals. We should not think that we are men and women. but only that we are human beings, born to cherish and to help one another. No sooner are a young man and a young woman left alone than he pays compliments to her, and perhaps before he takes a wife, he has courted two hundred women. Bah! If I belonged to the marrying set, I could find a woman to love without all that!

When I was in India and saw these things from the outside, I was told it was all right, it was mere pleasantry and I believed it. But I have travelled since then, and I know it is not right. It is wrong, only you of the West shut your eyes and call it good. The trouble with the nations of the West is that they are young, foolish, fickle, and wealthy. What mischief can come of one of these qualities; but when all three, all four, are combined beware!

If you have burning faith and all-conquering love and almighty purity, I do not doubt that you will shortly succeed. o not take any hasty step. First purify yourself by work and devotion.

Infinite patience, infinite purity, and infinite perseverance are the secret of success in a good cause.

External purification is keeping the body pure; a dirty man will never be a Yogi. There must be internal purification also. Internal purity is of greater value than external, but both are necessary, and external purity, without internal, is of no good.

I for one will give anything to get rid of the last lingering bit of Oriental formality in me and speak out like a child of nature. Oh, to live even for a day in the full light of freedom, to breathe the free air of simplicity! Is not that the highest purity?

Is there a greater strength than that of Brahmacharya—purity, my boy?

If theology and dogma stand in your way in search of truth, put them aside. Learn to think without prejudice, to love all beings for love's sake, to express your convictions fearlessly, to lead a life of purity, and the sunlight of truth will illuminate you.

The conditions necessary for the taught are purity, a real thirst after knowledge, and perseverance. No impure soul can be really religious. Purity in thought, speech, and act is absolutely necessary for any one to be religious.

Note here the conditions of imparting the truth. First, the purity—a boy, a pure, unclouded soul, asking the secret of the universe. Second, that he must take truth for truth's sake alone. Until the truth has come through one who has had realisation, from one who has perceived it himself, it cannot become fruitful. Books cannot give it, argument cannot establish it. Truth comes unto him who knows the secret of it.

Those who give themselves up to the Lord do more for the world than all the so-called workers. One man who has purified himself thoroughly accomplishes more than a regiment of preachers. Out of purity and silence comes the word of power.

Do not fight with people; do not antagonise anyone. Why should we mind if Jack and John become Christians? Let them follow whatever religion suits them. Why should you mix in controversies? Bear with the various opinions of everybody. Patience, purity, and perseverance will prevail.

Purity is absolutely the basic work, the bed-rock upon which the whole Bhakti-building rests. Cleansing the external body and discriminating the food are both easy, but without internal cleanliness and purity, these external observances are of no value whatsoever. In the list of qualities conducive to purity, as given by Ramanuja, there are enumerated, Satya, truthfulness; Ârjava, sincerity; Dayâ, doing good to others without any gain to one's self; Ahimsâ, not injuring others by thought, word, or deed; Anabhidhyâ, not coveting others' goods, not thinking vain thoughts, and not brooding over injuries received from another.

In this list, the one idea that deserves special notice is Ahimsa, non-injury to others. This duty of non-injury is, so to speak, obligatory on us in relation to all beings. As with some, it does not simply mean the non-injuring of human beings and mercilessness towards the lower animals; nor, as with some others, does it mean the protecting of cats and dogs and feeding of ants with sugar — with liberty to injure brother-man in every horrible way! It is remarkable that almost every good idea in this world can be carried to a disgusting extreme. A good practice carried to an extreme and worked in accordance with the letter of the law becomes a positive evil. The stinking monks of certain religious sects, who do not bathe lest the vermin on their bodies should be killed, never think of the discomfort and disease they bring to their fellow human beings. They do not, however, belong to the religion of the Vedas!

The Vedas teach that the soul is divine, only held in the bondage of matter; perfection will be reached when this bond will burst, and the word they use for it is therefore, Mukti — freedom, freedom from the bonds of imperfection, freedom from death and misery.

And this bondage can only fall off through the mercy of God, and this mercy comes on the pure. So purity is the condition of His mercy. How does that mercy act? He reveals Himself to the pure heart; the pure and the stainless see God, yea, even in this life; then and then only all the crookedness of the heart is made straight. Then all doubt ceases. He is no more the freak of a terrible law of causation. This is the very centre, the very vital conception of Hinduism. The Hindu does not want to live upon words and theories. If there are existences beyond the ordinary sensuous existence, he wants to come face to face with them. If there is a soul in him which is not matter, if there is an all-merciful universal Soul, he will go to Him direct. He must see Him, and that alone can destroy all doubts. So the best proof a Hindu sage gives about the soul, about God, is: "I have seen the soul; I have seen God." And that is the only condition of perfection. The Hindu religion does not consist in struggles and attempts to believe a certain doctrine or dogma, but in realising — not in believing, but in being and becoming.

Thus the whole object of their system is by constant struggle to become perfect, to become divine, to reach God and see God, and this reaching God, seeing God, becoming perfect even as the Father in Heaven is perfect, constitutes the religion of the Hindus.

If your mind be not pure and you try to follow Yoga, you will perhaps attain some supernatural power, but that will be a hindrance. Purity of mind is the first thing necessary.

. . . Purity, patience, and perseverance overcome all obstacles. All great things must of necessity be slow.

The soul in itself is perfect. The Old Testament of the Hebrews admits man perfect at the beginning. Man made himself impure by his own actions. But he is to regain his old nature, his pure nature. Some speak of these things in allegories, fables, and symbols. But when we begin to analyse these statements, we find that they all teach that the human soul is in its very nature perfect, and that man is to regain that original purity. How? By knowing God. Just as the Bible says, "No man can see God but through the Son." What is meant by it? That seeing God is the aim and goal of all human life. The sonship must come before we become one with the Father. Remember that man lost his purity through his own actions. When we suffer, it is because of our own acts; God is not to be blamed for it.

Remember that perfect purity, disinterestedness, and obedience to the Guru are the secret of all success.

Sincerity of conviction and purity of motive will surely gain the day; and even a small minority, armed with these, is surely destined to prevail against all odds.

Strength is in goodness, in purity.

The man who is groping through sin, through misery, the man who is choosing the path through hells, will reach it, but it will take time. We cannot save him. Some hard knocks on his head will help him to turn to the Lord. The path of virtue, purity, unselfishness, spirituality, becomes known at last and what all are doing unconsciously, we are trying to do consciously.

The idea is expressed by St. Paul, "The God that ye ignorantly worship, Him declare I unto you." This is the lesson for the whole world to learn. What have these philosophies and theories of nature to do, if not to help us to attain to this one goal in life? Let us come to that consciousness of the identity of everything and let man see himself in everything. Let us be no more the worshippers of creeds or sects with small limited notions of God, but see Him in everything in the universe. If you are knowers of God, you will everywhere find the same worship as in your own heart.

A condition necessary in the teacher is sinlessness. The question is often asked, "Why should we look into the character and personality of a teacher? We have only to judge of what he says, and take that up." This is not right. If a man wants to teach me something of dynamics, or chemistry, or any other physical science, he may be anything he likes, because what the physical sciences require is merely an intellectual equipment; but in the spiritual sciences it is impossible from first to last that there can be any spiritual light in the soul that is impure. What religion can an impure man teach? The sine qua non of acquiring spiritual truth for one's self or for imparting it to others is the purity of heart and soul.

A vision of God or a glimpse of the beyond never comes until the soul is pure. Hence with the teacher of religion we must see first what he is , and then what he says. He must be perfectly pure, and then alone comes the value of his words, because he is only then the true "transmitter". What can he transmit if he has not spiritual power in himself? There must be the worthy vibration of spirituality in the mind of the teacher, so that it may be sympathetically conveyed to the mind of the taught. The function of the teacher is indeed an affair of the transference of something, and not one of mere stimulation of the existing intellectual or other faculties in the taught. Something real and appreciable as an influence comes from the teacher and goes to the taught. Therefore the teacher must be pure.

The soul by its [very] nature is blessed, pure, and perfect; it could never be pure if its nature was impure. The soul's nature is purity; that is why souls [can] become pure. It is blessed [by nature]; that is why it [can] become blessed. It is peace; [that is why it can become peaceful].

All of us who find ourselves in this plane, attracted to the body, work hard for a living, with jealousies and quarrels and hardships, and then death. That shows we are not what we should be. We are not free, perfectly pure, and so on. The soul, as it were, has become degraded. Then what the soul requires is expansion.

"Good and bad deeds are not the direct causes in the transformations of nature, but they act as breakers of obstacles to the evolutions of nature: as a farmer breaks the obstacles to the course of water, which then runs down by its own nature." Here Patanjali gives the celebrated example of the cultivator bringing water into his field from a huge tank somewhere. The tank is already filled and the water would flood his land in a moment, only there is a mud-wall between the tank and his field. As soon as the barrier is broken, in rushes the water out of its own power and force. This mass of power and purity and perfection is in the soul already. The only difference is the Âvarana — this veil — that has been cast over it. Once the veil is removed, the soul attains to purity, and its powers become manifest.

This, you ought to remember, is the great difference between Eastern and Western thought. Hence you find people teaching such awful doctrines as that we are all born sinners, and because we do not believe in such awful doctrines we are all born wicked. They never stop to think that if we are by our very nature wicked, we can never be good — for how can nature change? If it changes, it contradicts itself; it is not nature. We ought to remember this. Here the dualist, and the Advaitist, and all others in India agree.

The work of ethics has been, and will be in the future, not the destruction of variation and the establishment of sameness in the external world — which is impossible for it would bring death and annihilation — but to recognise the unity in spite of all these variations, to recognise the God within, in spite of everything that frightens us, to recognise that infinite strength as the property of everyone in spite of all apparent weakness, and to recognise the eternal, infinite, essential purity of the soul in spite of everything to the contrary that appears on the surface. This we have to recognise. Taking one side alone, one half only of the position, is dangerous and liable to lead to quarrels. We must take the whole thing as it is, stand on it as our basis and work it out in every part of our lives, as individuals and as unit members of society.

Was it not purity and unselfish labour that made sages like Manu and Yajnavalkya, or was it something else? Well, we ourselves can be far greater than even Manu and Yajnavalkya if we try to; why will not our views prevail then?

We hear much about brutal husbands all over the world and about the impurity of men, but is it not true that there are quite as many brutal and impure women as men? If all women were as good and pure as their own constant assertions would lead one to believe, I am perfectly satisfied that there would not be one impure man in the world. What brutality is there which purity and chastity cannot conquer?

Be you holy and, above all, sincere; and do not for a moment give up your trust in the Lord, and you will see the light. Whatever is truth will remain for ever; whatever is not, none can preserve. We are helped in being born in a time when everything is quickly searched out. Whatever others think or do, lower not your standard of purity, morality, and love of God; above all, beware of all secret organisations. No one who loves God need fear any jugglery. Holiness is the highest and divinest power in earth and in heaven. "Truth alone triumphs, not untruth. Through truth alone is opened the way to God" (Mundaka, III. i. 6).

Never quarrel about religion. All quarrels and disputations concerning religion simply show that spirituality is not present. Religious quarrels are always over the husks. When purity, when spirituality goes, leaving the soul dry, quarrels begin, and not before.

The Vedantin thinker boldly says that the enjoyments in this life, even the most degraded joys, are but manifestations of that One Divine Bliss, the Essence of the Soul.

This idea seems to be the most prominent in Vedanta, and, as I have said, it appears to me that every religion holds it. I have yet to know the religion which does not. It is the one universal idea working through all religions You find there the allegorical statement that the first man Adam was pure, and that his purity was obliterated by his evil deeds afterwards. It is clear from this allegory that they thought that the nature of the primitive man was perfect. The impurities that we see, the weaknesses that we feel, are but superimpositions on that nature, and the subsequent history of the Christian religion shows that they also believe in the possibility, nay, the certainty of regaining that old state.

his is the whole history of the Bible, Old and New Testaments together. So with the Mohammedans: they also believed in Adam and the purity of Adam, and through Mohammed the way was opened to regain that lost state. So with the Buddhists: they believe in the state called Nirvana which is beyond this relative world. It is exactly the same as the Brahman of the Vedantins, and the whole system of the Buddhists is founded upon the idea of regaining that lost state of Nirvana.

Be pure first, and you will have power. Simply saying, "I am a Rishi", will not do; but when you are a Rishi you will find that others obey you instinctively. Something mysterious emanates from you, which makes them follow you, makes them hear you, makes them unconsciously, even against their will, carry out your plans. That is Rishihood.

Truth, purity, and unselfishness — wherever these are present, there is no power below or above the sun to crush the possessor thereof. Equipped with these, one individual is able to face the whole universe in opposition.

On the Math

(From the Diary of Shri Sharat Chandra Chakravarty. Swamiji framed certain rules for the guidance of the Sannyasins and Brahmacharins of the Math, the object of which was to keep them from indiscriminate mixing with worldly people.)

Swamiji: Nowadays I feel a peculiar smell of lax self-control in the dress and clothes of worldly people; therefore I have made it a rule in the Math that householders should not sit or lie on the beds of Sadhus. Formerly I used to read in the Shastras that such a smell is felt, and therefore Sannyasins cannot bear the smell of householders. Now I see it is true. By strictly observing the rules that have been framed, the Brahmacharins will in time grow into genuine Sannyasins. When they are established in the ideal of Sannyasa, they will be able to mix on an equal footing with worldly men without any harm. But now if they are not kept within the barriers of strict rules, they will all go wrong. In order to attain to ideal Brahmacharya one has in the beginning to observe strict rules regarding chastity. Not only should one keep oneself strictly aloof from the least association with the opposite sex, but also give up the company of married people even.

Disciple: Sir, I feel more intimacy with the Math and its inmates than with my own family. As if they are known to me from a long long time. The unbounded freedom that I enjoy in the Math, I feel nowhere else in the world."

Swamiji: All those who are pure in spirit will feel like that here. Those who do not feel so must be taken as not belonging to this Math and its ideals. That is the reason why many people come here out of mere sensation-mongering and then run away. Those who are devoid of continence and are running after money day and night will never be able to appreciate the ideals of the Math, nor regard the Math people as their own. The Sannyasins of this Math are not like those of old, ash-besmeared, with matted hair and iron tongs in their hands, and curing disease by medicinal titbits; therefore seeing the contrast, people cannot appreciate them. The ways, movements and ideas of our Master were all cast in a new mould, so we are also of a new type. Sometimes dressed like gentlemen, we are engaged in lecturing; at other times, throwing all aside, with " Hara, Hara, Vyom Vyom " on the lips, ash-clad, we are immersed in meditation and austerities in mountains and forests.

Now it won't do to merely quote the authority of our ancient books. The tidal wave of Western civilisation is now rushing over the length and breadth of the country. It won't do now simply to sit in meditation on mountain tops without realising in the least its usefulness. Now is wanted — as said in the Gita by the Lord — intense Karma-Yoga, with unbounded courage and indomitable strength in the heart. Then only will the people of the country be roused, otherwise they will continue to be as much in the dark as you are.

Unbroken Brahmacharya Is The Secret Of Power

(Conversation with Shri Priya Nath Sinha, translated from Bengali)

Myself: Well, Swamiji, in your lectures in the West you have frequently and eloquently dwelt on our characteristic talents and virtues, and many convincing proofs you have put forward to show our whole-souled love of religion; but now you say that we have become full of Tamas; and at the same time you are accrediting us as the teachers of the eternal religion of the Rishis to the world! How is that?

Swamiji: Do you mean to say that I should go about from country to country, expatiating on your failings before the public? Should I not rather hold up before them the characteristic virtues that mark you as a nation? It is always good to tell a man his defects in a direct way and in a friendly spirit to make him convinced of them, so that he may correct himself — but you should trumpet forth his virtues before others. Shri Ramakrishna used to say that if you repeatedly tell a bad man that he is good, he turns in time to be good; similarly, a good man becomes bad if he is incessantly called so. There, in the West, I have said enough to the people of their shortcomings. Mind, up to my time, all who went over to the West from our country have sung paeans to them in praise of their virtues and have trumpeted out only our blemishes to their ears. Consequently, it is no wonder that they have learnt to hate us. For this reason I have laid before them your virtues, and pointed out to them their vices, just as I am now telling you of your weaknesses and their good points. However full of Tamas you may have become, something of the nature of the ancient Rishis, however little it may be, is undoubtedly in you still — at least the framework of it. But that does not show that one should be in a hurry to take up at once the role of a teacher of religion and go over to the West to preach it. First of all, one must completely mould one's religious life in solitude, must be perfect in renunciation and must preserve Brahmacharya without a break. The Tamas has entered into you — what of that? Cannot the Tamas be destroyed? It can be done in less than no time! It was for the destruction of this Tamas that Bhagavân Shri Ramakrishna came to us.

Myself: But who can aspire to be like you, Swamiji ?

Swamiji: Do you think that there will be no more Vivekanandas after I die! That batch of young men who came and played music before me a little while ago, whom you all despise for being addicted to intoxicating drugs and look upon as worthless fellows, if the Lord wishes, each and everyone of them may become a Vivekananda! There will be no lack of Vivekanandas, if the world needs them — thousands and millions of Vivekanandas will appear — from where, who knows! Know for certain that the work done by me is not the work of Vivekananda, it is His work — the Lord's own work! If one governor-general retires, another is sure to be sent in his place by the Emperor. Enveloped in Tamas however much you may be, know all that will clear away if you take refuge in Him by being sincere to the core of your heart. The time is opportune now, as the physician of the world-disease has come. Taking His name, if you set yourself to work, He will accomplish everything Himself through you. Tamas itself will be transformed into the highest Sattva!

Myself: Whatever you may say, I cannot bring myself to believe in these words. Who can come by that oratorical power of expounding philosophy which you have?

Swamiji: You don't know! That power may come to all. That power comes to him who observes unbroken Brahmacharya for a period of twelve years, with the sole object of realising God. I have practiced that kind of Brahmacharya myself, and so a screen has been removed, as it were, from my brain. For that reason, I need not any more think over or prepare myself for any lectures on such a subtle subject as philosophy. Suppose I have to lecture tomorrow; all that I shall speak about will pass tonight before my eyes like so many pictures; and the next day I put into words during my lecture all those things that I saw. So you will understand now that it is not any power which is exclusively my own. Whoever will practice unbroken Brahmacharya for twelve years will surely have it. If you do so, you too will get it. Our Shâstras do not say that only such and such a person will get it and not others!

Myself: Do you remember, Swamiji, one day, before you took Sannyâsa, we were sitting in the house of —, and you were trying to explain the mystery of Samâdhi to us. And when I called in question the truth of your words, saying that Samadhi was not possible in this Kali Yuga, you emphatically demanded: "Do you want to see Samadhi or to have it yourself? I get Samadhi myself, and I can make you have it! " No sooner had you finished saying so than a stranger came up and we did not pursue that subject any further.

Swamiji: Yes, I remember the occasion.

Later, on my pressing him to make me get Samadhi, he said, "You see, having continually lectured and worked hard for several years, the quality of Rajas has become too predominant in me. Hence that power is lying covered, as it were, in me now. If I leave all work and go to the Himalayas and meditate in solitude for some time, then that power will again come out in me."

Brahmacharya and Women

As sons should be married after observing Brahmacharya up to the thirtieth year, so daughters also must observe Brahmacharya and be educated by their parents. But what are we actually doing? Can you better the condition of your women? Then there will be hope for your well-being. Otherwise you will remain as backward as you are now.

(Vivekananda was asked, "Surely the religious exaltation of Brahmacharya, by taking the highest place from the mother and wife and giving it to those who evade those relations, is a direct blow dealt at woman?"

This is Vivekananda reply.)

"You should remember that if religion exalts Brahmacharya for woman, it does exactly the same for man. Moreover, your question shows a certain confusion in your own mind. Hinduism indicates one duty, only one, for the human soul. It is to seek to realise the permanent amidst the evanescent. No one presumes to point out any one way in which this may be done. Marriage or non-marriage, good or evil, learning or ignorance, any of these is justified, if it leads to the goal. In this respect lies the great contrast between it and Buddhism, for the latter's outstanding direction is to realise the impermanence of the external, which, broadly speaking, can only be done in one way. Do you recall the story of the young Yogi in the Mahâbhârata who prided himself on his psychic powers by burning the bodies of a crow and crane by his intense will, produced by anger? Do you remember that the young saint went into the town and found first a wife nursing her sick husband and then the butcher Dharma-Vyâdha, both of whom had obtained enlightenment in the path of common faithfulness and duty?

To the women of this country, I would say exactly what I say to the men. Believe in India and in our Indian faith. Be strong and hopeful and unashamed, and remember that with something to take, Hindus have immeasurably more to give than any other people in the world.

Abstinence

All the criticism against the Advaita philosophy can be summed up in this, that it does not conduce to sense-enjoyments; and we are glad to admit that.

Competitions for life or sex-gratification are only momentary, unnecessary, extraneous effects, caused by ignorance.

Give up the idea of sex and possessions. There is no other bond. Marriage and sex and money the only living devils. All earthly love proceeds from the body. No sex, no possessions; as these fall off, the eyes open to spiritual vision. The soul regains its own infinite power. How I wish I were in England to see Harriet. I have one wish left — to see you four sisters before I die, and that must happen.

In my first speech in this country, in Chicago, I addressed that audience as 'Sisters and Brothers of America', and you know that they all rose to their feet. You may wonder what made them do this, you may wonder if I had some strange power. Let me tell you that I did have a power and this is it — never once in my life did I allow myself to have even one sexual thought. I trained my mind, my thinking, and the powers that man usually uses along that line I put into a higher channel, and it developed a force so strong that nothing could resist it.

Sex – love and creation! These are at the root of most religions. And these in India are called Vaishnavism, and in the West Christianity. How few have dared to worship Death or Kali! Let us worship Death! Let us embrace the Terrible, because it is terrible, not asking that it be toned down. Let us take misery for misery's own sake!

Shri Chaitanya was a man of tremendous renunciation and had nothing to do with woman and carnal appetites. But, in later times, his disciples admitted women into their order, mixed indiscriminately with them in his name, and made an awful mess of the whole thing. And the ideal of love which the Lord exemplified in his life was perfectly selfless and bereft of any vestige of lust; that sexless love can never be the property of the masses. But the subsequent Vaishnava Gurus, instead of laying particular stress first on the aspect of renunciation in the Master's life, bestowed all their zeal on preaching and infusing his ideal of love among the masses, and the consequence was that the common people could not grasp and assimilate that high ideal of divine love, and naturally made of it the worst form of love between man and woman.

The highest love is the love that is sexless, for it is perfect unity that is expressed in the highest love, and sex differentiates bodies. It is therefore only in spirit that union is possible. The less we have of the physical idea, the more perfect will be our love; at last all physical thought will be forgotten, and the two souls will become one. We love, love always. Love comes and penetrates through the forms and sees beyond. It has been said, "The lover sees Helen's beauty in an Ethiopian's brow." The Ethiopian is the suggestion and upon that suggestion the man throws his love. As the oyster throws over the irritants, it finds in its shell, the substance that turns the irritants into beautiful pearls, so man throws out love, and it is always man's highest ideal that he loves, and the highest ideal is always selfless; so man loves love. God is love, and we love God—or love love. We only see love, love cannot be expressed. "A dumb man eating butter" cannot tell you what butter is like. Butter is butter, and its qualities cannot be expressed to those who have not tasted it. Love for love's sake cannot be expressed to those who have not felt it.

The nerve centre at the base of the spine near the sacrum is most important. It is the seat of the generative substance of the sexual energy and is symbolised by the Yogi as a triangle containing a tiny serpent coiled up in it. This sleeping serpent is called Kundalini, and to raise this Kundalini is the whole object of Raja – yoga.

The great sexual force, raised from animal action and sent upward to the great dynamo of the human system, the brain, and there stored up, becomes Ojas or spiritual force. All good thought, all prayer, resolves a part of that animal energy into Ojas and helps to give us spiritual power. This Ojas is the real man and in human beings alone is it possible for this storage of Ojas to be accomplished. One in whom the whole animal sex force has been transformed into Ojas is a god. He speaks with power, and his words regenerate the world.

The Yogi pictures this serpent as being slowly lifted from stage to stage until the highest, the pineal gland, is reached. No man or woman can be really spiritual until the sexual energy, the highest power possessed by man, has been converted into Ojas.

The Yogis claim that of all the energies that are in the human body the highest is what they call "Ojas". Now this Ojas is stored up in the brain, and the more Ojas is in a man's head, the more powerful he is, the more intellectual, the more spiritually strong. One man may speak beautiful language and beautiful thoughts, but they, do not impress people; another man speaks neither beautiful language nor beautiful thoughts, yet his words charm. Every movement of his is powerful. That is the power of Ojas.

Now in every man there is more or less of this Ojas stored up. All the forces that are working in the body in their highest become Ojas. You must remember that it is only a question of transformation. The same force which is working outside as electricity or magnetism will become changed into inner force; the same forces that are working as muscular energy will be changed into Ojas. The Yogis say that that part of the human energy which is expressed as sex energy, in sexual thought, when checked and controlled, easily becomes changed into Ojas, and as the Muladhara guides these, the Yogi pays particular attention to that centre. He tries to take up all his sexual energy and convert it into Ojas. It is only the chaste man or woman who can make the Ojas rise and store it in the brain; that is why chastity has always been considered the highest virtue. A man feels that if he is unchaste, spirituality goes away, he loses mental vigour and moral stamina. That is why in all the religious orders in the world which have produced spiritual giants you will always find absolute chastity insisted upon. That is why the monks came into existence, giving up marriage. There must be perfect chastity in thought, word, and deed; without it the practice of Raja-Yoga is dangerous, and may lead to insanity. If people practice Raja-Yoga and at the same time lead an impure life, how can they expect to become Yogis?

The "Ojas" is that which makes the difference between man and man. The man who has much Ojas is the leader of men. It gives a tremendous power of attraction. Ojas is manufactured from the nerve-currents. It has this peculiarity: it is most easily made from that force which manifests itself in the sexual powers. If the powers of the sexual centres are not frittered away and their energies wasted (action is only thought in a grosser state), they can be manufactured into Ojas.

The circle of vision has become so narrow, so degraded, so beastly, so animal! None is desiring anything beyond this body. Oh, the terrible degradation, the terrible misery of it! What little flesh, the five senses, the stomach! What is the world but a combination of stomach and sex? Look at millions of men and women — that is what they are living for. Take these away from them and they will find their life empty, meaningless, and intolerable. Such are we. And such is our mind; it is continually hankering for ways and means to satisfy the hunger of the stomach and sex. All the time this is going on. There is also endless suffering; these desires of the body bring only momentary satisfaction and endless suffering. It is like drinking a cup of which the surface layer is nectar, while underneath all is poison. But we still hanker for all these things.

Jealousy

Avoid jealousy and selfishness. Be obedient and eternally faithful to the cause of truth, humanity, and your country, and you will move the world. Remember it is the person, the life, which is the secret of power — nothing else. Jealousy is the bane of all slaves. It is the bane of our nation. Avoid that always.

Ay, for ages we have been saturated with awful jealousy; we are always getting jealous of each other. Why has this man a little precedence, and not I? Even in the worship of God we want precedence, to such a state of slavery have we come. This is to be avoided. If there is any crying sin in India at this time it is this slavery. Every one wants to command, and no one wants to obey; and this is owing to the absence of that wonderful Brahmacharya system of yore.

First, learn to obey. The command will come by itself. Always first learn to be a servant, and then you will be fit to be a master. Avoid this jealousy and you will do great works that have yet to be done. Our ancestors did most wonderful works, and we look back upon their work with veneration and pride. But we also are going to do great deeds, and let others look back with blessings and pride upon us as their ancestors. With the blessing of the Lord every one here will yet do such deeds that will eclipse those of our ancestors, great and glorious as they may have been.

Brother, we can get rid of everything, but not of that cursed jealousy. That is a national sin with us, speaking ill of others, and burning at heart at the greatness of others. Mine alone is the greatness, none else should rise to it!

How difficult it is to look through each other's eyes, and that is the bane of humanity. That is the basis of hatred and jealousy, of quarrel and of fight.

Hold on with faith and strength; be true, be honest, be pure, and don't quarrel among yourselves. Jealousy is the bane of our race.

Give up jealousy and conceit. Learn to work unitedly for others. This is the great need of our country.

I see persons giving me almost the whole of their love. But I must not give anyone the whole of mine in return, for that day the work would be ruined. Yet there are some who will look for such a return, not having the breadth of the impersonal view.

It is absolutely necessary to the work that I should have the enthusiastic love of as many as possible, while I myself remain entirely impersonal. Otherwise jealousy and quarrels would break up everything.

A leader must be impersonal. I am sure you understand this. I do not mean that one should be a brute, making use of the devotion of others for his own ends, and laughing in his sleeve meanwhile. What I mean is what I am, intensely personal in my love, but having the power to pluck out my own heart with my own hand, if it becomes necessary, "for the good of many, for the welfare of many", as Buddha said. Madness of love, and yet in it no bondage. Matter changed into spirit by the force of love. Nay, that is the gist of our Vedanta.

Jealousy is the central vice of every enslaved race. And it is jealousy and want of combination which cause and perpetuate slavery.

Let us wipe off first that mark which nature always puts on the forehead of a slave — the stain of jealousy. Be jealous of none. Be ready to lend a hand to every worker of good. Send a good thought for every being in the three worlds.

There should be no jealousy in regard to objects of the senses. Jealousy is the root of all evil, and a most difficult thing to conquer.

Our people have no idea, no appreciation. On the other hand, that horrible jealousy and suspicious nature which is the natural outcome of a thousand years of slavery make them stand as enemies to every new idea.

Strike the iron while it is hot. Idleness won't do. Throw overboard all idea of jealousy and egotism, once for all. Come on to the practical field with tremendous energy; to work, in the fullness of strength! As to the rest, the Lord will point out the way. The whole world will be deluged by a tidal wave.

Work, work, work — let this be your motto. I cannot see anything else. There is no end of work here — I am careering all over the country. Wherever the seed of his power will find its way, there it will fructify — आद्य वा अब्दशतान्ते वा—be it today, or in a hundred years."

You are all of infinite strength — how long does it take you to keep off petty jealousy or egoistic ideas! The moment such propensity comes, resign yourselves to the Lord! Just make over your body and mind to His work, and all troubles will be at an end for ever.

You must know once for all, I am born without jealousy, without avarice, without the desire to rule — whatever other vices I am born with I never had any jealousy about what friends you made.

I never criticised my brethren for mixing up in anything. Only I do believe the Western people have the peculiarity of trying to force upon others whatever seems good to them, forgetting that what is good for you may not be good for others. As such, I am afraid you might try to force upon others whatever turn your mind might take in contact with new friends. That was the only reason I sometimes tried to stop any particular influence, and nothing else. (In a letter written to Sister Nivedita, dated 25 August 1900).

Sacrifice

In the animal kingdom we really see such laws as struggle for existence, survival of the fittest, etc., evidently at work. Therefore Darwin's theory seems true to a certain extent. But in the human kingdom, where there is the manifestation of rationality, we find just the reverse of those laws.

For instance, in those whom we consider really great men or ideal characters, we scarcely observe any external struggle. In the animal kingdom instinct prevails; but the more a man advances, the more he manifests rationality.

For this reason, progress in the rational human kingdom cannot be achieved, like that in the animal kingdom, by the destruction of others! The highest evolution of man is effected through sacrifice alone. A man is great among his fellows in proportion as he can sacrifice for the sake of others, while in the lower strata of the animal kingdom, that animal is the strongest which can kill the greatest number of animals.

Hence the struggle theory is not equally applicable to both kingdoms. Man's struggle is in the mental sphere. A man is greater in proportion as he can control his mind. When the mind's activities are perfectly at rest, the Atman manifests Itself.

The struggle which we observe in the animal kingdom for the preservation of the gross body obtains in the human plane of existence for gaining mastery over the mind or for attaining the state of balance. Like a living tree and its reflection in the water of a tank, we find opposite kinds of struggle in the animal and human kingdoms.

Do all as a sacrifice or offering to the Lord. Be in the world, but not of it, like the lotus leaf whose roots are in the mud but which remains always pure. Let your love go to all, whatever they do to you.

A blind man cannot see colour, so how can we see evil unless it is in us? We compare what we see outside with what we find in ourselves and pronounce judgment accordingly. Do not want this world, because what you desire you get.

Seek the Lord and the Lord only. The more power there is, the more bondage, the more fear. How much more afraid and miserable are we than the ant! Get out of it all and come to the Lord. Seek the science of the maker and not that of the made.

Great things can be done by great sacrifices only. No selfishness, no name, no fame, yours or mine, nor my Master's even! Work, work the idea, the plan, my boys, my brave, noble, good souls — to the wheel, to the wheel put your shoulders!

Stop not to look back for name, or fame, or any such nonsense. Throw self overboard and work. Remember, "The grass when made into a rope by being joined together can even chain a mad elephant."

The Lord's blessings on you all! His power be in you all— as I believe it is already . "Wake up, stop not until the goal is reached", say the Vedas.

Where is that martial spirit which, at the very outset, requires one to know how to serve and obey and to practise self-restraint! The martial spirit is not self – assertion but self – sacrifice. One must be ready to advance and lay down one's life at the word of command, before he can command the hearts and lives of others. One must sacrifice himself first.

I know, and know for sure, that great things are done only by great sacrifices. I know for certain that India requires the sacrifice of her highest and best.

Throughout the history of the world you find great men make great sacrifices and the mass of mankind enjoy the benefit. If you want to give up everything for your own salvation, it is nothing. Do you want to forgo even your own salvation for the good of the world? You are God, think of that.

I want a band of young Bengalis — who alone are the hope of this country. My hope of the future lies in the youths of character — intelligent, renouncing all for the service of others, and obedient — who can sacrifice their lives in working out my ideas and thereby do good to themselves and the country at large.

Otherwise, boys of the common run are coming in groups and will come. Dullness is written on their faces — their hearts are devoid of energy, their bodies feeble and unfit for work, and minds devoid of courage. What work will be done by these? If I get ten or twelve boys with the faith of Nachiketâ, I can turn the thoughts and pursuits of this country in a new channel.

First, we have to understand the ideal, and then the methods by which we can make it practical. Those of you who are Sannyasins must try to do good to others, for Sannyasa means that.

There is no time to deliver a long discourse on “Renunciation”, but I shall very briefly characterise it as “the love of death “. Worldly people love life. The Sannyasin is to love death.

Are we to commit suicide then? Far from it. For suicides are not lovers of death, as it is often seen that when a man trying to commit suicide fails, he never attempts it for a second time.

What is the love of death then? We must die, that is certain; let us die then for a good cause. Let all our actions — eating, drinking, and everything that we do — tend towards the sacrifice of our self.

You nourish your body by eating. What good is there in doing that if you do not hold it as a sacrifice to the well-being of others? You nourish your minds by reading books. There is no good in doing that unless you hold it also as a sacrifice to the whole world. For the whole world is one; you are rated a very insignificant part of it, and therefore it is right for you that you should serve your millions of brothers rather than aggrandise this little self.

Thus you must die a gradual death. In such a death is heaven, all good is stored therein — and in its opposite is all that is diabolical and evil.

Then as to the methods of carrying the ideals into practical life. First, we have to understand that we must not have any impossible ideal. An ideal which is too high makes a nation weak and degraded. This happened after the Buddhistic and the Jain reforms.

On the other hand, too much practicality is also wrong. If you have not even a little imagination, if you have no ideal let guide you, you are simply a brute. So we must not lower our ideal, neither are we to lose sight of practicality. We must avoid the two extremes.

Let us be at peace, perfect peace, with ourselves, and give up our whole body and mind and everything as an eternal sacrifice unto the Lord. Instead of the sacrifice of pouring oblations into the fire, perform this one great sacrifice day and night — the sacrifice of your little self.

"In search of wealth in this world, Thou art the only wealth I have found; I sacrifice myself unto Thee. In search of some one to be loved, Thou art the only one beloved I have found; I sacrifice myself unto Thee."

Let us repeat this day and night, and say, “Nothing for me; no matter whether the thing is good, bad, or indifferent; I do not care for it; I sacrifice all unto Thee.”

Day and night let us renounce our seeming self until it becomes a habit with us to do so, until it gets into the blood, the nerves, and the brain, and the whole body is every moment obedient to this idea of self-renunciation. Go then into the midst of the battlefield, with the roaring cannon and the din of war, and you will find yourself to be free and at peace.

No great thing can be done without sacrifice. Who on seeing the tiny sprout of the banyan can imagine that in course of time it will develop into a gigantic banyan tree?The heart must be plucked out and the bleeding heart placed upon the altar.

Then great things are done. Is there any other way? None have found it. I appeal to each one of you, to those who have accomplished any great thing. Oh, how much it has cost! What agony! What torture! What terrible suffering is behind every deed of success in every life! You know that, all of you.

Nothing is gained except by sacrifice. he holiest function of our human consciousness, the noblest, do not make it unclean! Do not degrade it to the level of the brutes.... Make yourselves decent men! ... Be chaste and pure! ... There is no other way. Did Christ find any other way? ... If you can conserve and use the energy properly, it leads you to God. Inverted, it is hell itself

One idea that I see clear as daylight is that misery is caused by ignorance and nothing else. Who will give the world light? Sacrifice in the past has been the Law, it will be, alas, for ages to come. The earth's bravest and best will have to sacrifice themselves for the good of many, for the welfare of all. Buddhas by the hundred are necessary with eternal love and pity.

Religions of the world have become lifeless mockeries. What the world wants is character. The world is in need of those whose life is one burning love, selfless. That love will make every word tell like thunderbolt.

Sacrifice of everything for the good of others is real Sannyasa. They have never enjoyed any good thing in life. See how simple they are. Can you mitigate their misery a little? Otherwise, of what good is the wearing of the Gerua robe?

No great work can be done without sacrifice. The Purusha Himself sacrificed Himself to create this world. Lay down your comforts, your pleasures, your names, fame or position, nay even your lives, and make a bridge of human chains over which millions will cross this ocean of life.

Bring all the forces of good together. Do not care under what banner you march. Do not care what be your colour — green, blue, or red — but mix up all the colours and produce that intense glow of white, the colour of love. Ours is to work. The results will take care of themselves.

If any social institution stands in your way of becoming God, it will give way before the power of Spirit. I do not see into the future; nor do I care to see. But one vision I see dear as life before me: that the ancient Mother has awakened once more, sitting on Her throne rejuvenated, more glorious than ever. Proclaim Her to all the world with the voice of peace and benediction.

Sacrifice on God's altar earth's purest and best. He who struggles is better than he who never attempts. Even to look on one who has given up has a purifying effect. Stand up for God; let the world go. Have no compromise.

Give up the world, then alone you are loosened from the body. When it dies, you are âzâd , free. Be free. Death alone can never free us. Freedom must be attained by our own efforts during life; then, when the body falls, there will be no rebirth for the free.

The two great watchwords of every great religion are renunciation and self – sacrifice. We all want the truth, and we know that it must come, whether we want it or not. In a way we are all striving for that good. And what prevents our reaching it? It is ourselves. Your ancestors used to call it the devil; but it is our own false self.

We live in slavery, and we would die if we were out of it. We are like the man who lived in total darkness for ninety years and when taken out into the warm sunshine of nature, prayed to be taken back to his dungeon. You would not leave this old life to go into a newer and greater freedom which opens out.

Sacrifice your life for the good of others and go round to the doors of people carrying this message of fearlessness — arise, awake, and stop not till the goal is reached.

"सन्निमित्ते वरं त्यागो विनाशे नियते सति—When death is certain, it is best to sacrifice oneself for a good cause."

We must plunge heart and soul and body into the work. Until we be ready to sacrifice everything else to one Idea and to one alone, we never, never will see the light. Those that want to help mankind must take their own pleasure and pain, name and fame, and all sorts of interests, and make a bundle of them and throw them into the sea, and then come to the Lord.

This is what all the Masters said and did. Was it ever in the history of the world that any great work was done by the rich? It is the heart and the brain that do it ever and ever and not the purse.

My idea and all my life with it — and to God for help; to none else! This is the only secret of success.

The ideal law may be that no man should covet the belongings of others, but the actual law is that a very large number do. Thus the word law used in regard to laws of nature has a very different interpretation when applied to ethics and human actions generally.

Analysing the ethical laws of the world and comparing them with the actual state of things, two laws stand out supreme. The one, that of repelling everything from us—separating ourselves from everyone—which leads to self-aggrandisement even at the cost of everyone else's happiness.

The other, that of self-sacrifice—of taking no thought of ourselves—only of others. Both spring from the search for happiness—one, of finding happiness in injuring others and the ability of feeling that happiness only in our own senses. The other, of finding happiness in doing good to others —the ability of feeling happy, as it were, through the senses of others.

The great and good of the world are those who have the latter power predominating. Yet both these are working side by side conjointly; in almost everyone they are found in mixture, one or the other predominating. The thief steals, perhaps, for someone he loves.

When you have men who are ready to sacrifice their everything for their country, sincere to the backbone — when such men arise, India will become great in every respect. It is the men that make the country!

What is there in the country? If you catch the social morality and the political morality of the Japanese, you will be as great as they are. The Japanese are ready to sacrifice everything for their country, and they have become a great people. But you are not; you cannot be, you sacrifice everything only for your own families and possessions.

The Karma-Yogi wants everyone to be saved before himself. His only salvation is to help others to salvation. "To serve Krishna's servants is the highest worship." One great saint prayed, "Let me go to hell with the sins of the whole world, but let the world be saved." True worship leads to intense self – sacrifice.

What good is it carrying along a load of bones and flesh! Initiated into the Mantra of extreme self-sacrifice for the sake of God, go, lay down for others this body of flesh and bones like the Muni Dadhichi! Those alone, say the Shastras, are the real Gurus, who have studied the Vedas and the Vedanta, who are knowers of the Brahman, who are able to lead others beyond to fearlessness; when such are at hand, get yourself initiated, "no speculation in such a case". Do you know what has become of this principle now? — "like the blind leading the blind"!

Love must conquer hatred, hatred cannot conquer itself. Materialism and all its miseries can never be conquered by materialism. Armies when they attempt to conquer armies only multiply and make brutes of humanity. Spirituality must conquer the West.

Where are the men ready to go out to every country in the world with the messages of the great sages of India? Where are the men who are ready to sacrifice everything, so that this message shall reach every corner of the world? Such heroic spurs are wanted to help the spread of truth.

Such heroic workers are wanted to go abroad and help to disseminate the great truths of the Vedanta. The world wants it; without it the world will be destroyed. The whole of the Western world is on a volcano which may burst tomorrow, go to pieces tomorrow. They have searched every corner of the world and have found no respite. They have drunk deep of the cup of pleasure and found it vanity. Now is the time to work so that India's spiritual ideas may penetrate deep into the West.

Therefore young men of Madras, I specially ask you to remember this. We must go out, we must conquer the world through our spirituality and philosophy. There is no other alternative, we must do it or die. The only condition of national life, of awakened and vigorous national life, is the conquest of the world by Indian thought.

As by continuing our religious practices we gradually develop a certain determined tendency for it, so by performing disinterested work over and over again, even unwillingly, we gradually find the will merging itself in it. The inclination to work for others develops in this way, do you see? Just do some such work even though unwillingly, and then see if the actual fruit of Tapasya is realised within or not. As the outcome of work for the sake of others, the angularities of the mind get smoothed down, and men are gradually prepared for sincere self-sacrifice for the good of others.

As the outcome of work for the sake of others, the angularities of the mind get smoothed down, and men are gradually prepared for sincere self – sacrifice for the good of others.

We should feel the Eternal Unity so much, that we should weep for all sinners, knowing that it is we who are sinning. The eternal law is self – sacrifice, not self – assertion. What self to assert when all is one? There are no "rights", all is love.

The great truths that Jesus taught have never been lived. Let us try his method and see if the world will not be saved. The contrary method has nearly destroyed it. Selflessness only, not selfishness, can solve the question.

The idea of "right" is a limitation; there is really no "mine" and "thine", for I am thou and thou art I. We have "responsibility", not "rights".

We should say, "I am the universe", not "I am John" or "I am Mary". These limitations are all delusions and are what holds us in bondage, for as soon as I think, "I am John", I want exclusive posses sion of certain things and begin to say "me and mine", and continually make new distinctions in so doing.

So our bondage goes on increasing with every fresh distinction, and we get further and further away from the central Unity, the undivided Infinite. There is only one Individual, and each of us is That.

Oneness alone is love and fearlessness; separation leads us to hatred and fear. Oneness fulfils the law. Here, on earth, we strive to enclose little spaces and exclude outsiders, but we cannot do that in the sky, though that is what sectarian religion tries to do when it says, "Only this way leads to salvation, all others are wrong".

Our aim should be to wipe out these little enclosures to widen the boundaries until they are lost sight of, and to realise that all religions lead to God. This little puny self must be sacrificed. This is the truth symbolised by baptism into a new life, the death of the old man, the birth of the new — the perishing of the false self, the realisation of the Atman, the one Self of the universe.

It is more blessed, in my opinion, even to go wrong, impelled by one's free will and intelligence than to be good as an automaton. Again, can that be called society which is formed by an aggregate of men who are like lumps of clay, like lifeless machines, like heaped up pebbles?

How can such society fare well? Were good possible, then instead of being slaves for hundreds of years, we would have been the greatest nation on earth, and this soil of India, instead of being a mine of stupidity, would have been the eternal fountain-head of learning. Is not self-sacrifice, then, a virtue? Is it not the most virtuous deed to sacrifice the happiness of one, the welfare of one, for the sake of the many?

It is all a degeneration which has its root in selfishness. That in boarding a steamer one follows the vulgar maxim, "Uncle, save thy own precious skin", and in music and moments of recreation everyone tries to make a display of himself, is a typical picture of our mental state. Only a little training in self – sacrifice would take it away. It is the fault of the parents who do not teach their children good manners. Self – sacrifice, indeed, is the basis of all civilization.

Exactly, but as the Bengali adage goes, "Can beauty be manufactured by rubbing and scrubbing? Can love be generated by effort and compulsion?" What glory is there in the renunciation of an eternal beggar? What virtue is there in the sense- control of one devoid of sense-power?

What again is the self-sacrifice of one devoid of idea, devoid of heart, devoid of high ambition, and devoid of the conception of what constitutes society? What expression of devotedness to a husband is there by forcing a widow to commit Sati? Why make people do virtuous deeds by teaching superstitions?

I say, liberate, undo the shackles of people as much as you can. Can dirt be washed by dirt? Can bondage be removed by bondage? Where is the instance? When you would be able to sacrifice all desire for happiness for the sake of society, then you would be the Buddha, then you would be free: that is far off.

Again, do you think the way to do it lies through oppression? "Oh, what examples or self-denial are our widows! Oh, how sweet is child-marriage! Is another such custom possible! Can there be anything but love between husband and wife in such a marriage!" such is the whine going round nowadays.

But as to the men, the masters of the situation, there is no need of self-denial for them! Is there a virtue higher than serving others? But the same does not apply to Brâhmins — you others do it!

The truth is that in this country parents and relatives can ruthlessly sacrifice the best interests of their children and others for their own selfish ends to save themselves by compromise to society; and the teaching of generations rendering the mind callous has made it perfectly easy. He, the brave alone, can deny self. The coward, afraid of the lash, with one hand wipes his eyes and gives with the other.

Of what avail are such gifts? It is a far cry to love universal. The young plant should be hedged in and taken care of. One can hope gradually to attain to universal love if one can learn to love one object unselfishly. If devotion to one particular Ishta-Deva is attained, devotion to the universal Virat is gradually possible.

Therefore, when one has been able to deny self for an individual, one should talk of self-sacrifice for the sake of society, not before. It is action with desire that leads to action without desire. Is the renunciation of desire possible if desire did not exist in the beginning? And what could it mean? Can light have any meaning if there is no darkness?

Worship with desire, with attachment, comes first. Commence with the worship of the little, then the greater will come of itself.

Enjoyment

Whatever work we do, the mind is thrown into a wave, and after the work is finished, we think the wave is gone. No. It has only become fine, but it is still there. When we try to remember the work, it comes up again and becomes a wave. So it was there; if not, there would not have been memory.

Thus every action, every thought, good or bad, just goes down and becomes fine, and is there stored up. Both happy and unhappy thoughts are called pain-bearing obstructions, because according to the Yogis, they, in the long run, bring pain.

All happiness which comes from the senses will, eventually, bring pain. All enjoyment will make us thirst for more, and that brings pain as its result. There is no limit to man's desires; he goes on desiring, and when he comes to a point where desire cannot be fulfilled, the result is pain.

Therefore the Yogis regard the sum-total of the impressions, good or evil, as pain-bearing obstructions; they obstruct the way to freedom of the Soul.

The first ideal of the attempt to realise religion is that of renunciation. As far as we can, we must give up. Darkness and light, enjoyment of the world and enjoyment of God will never go together. "Ye cannot serve God and Mammon." Let people try it if they will, and I have seen millions in every country who have tried; but after all, it comes to nothing. If one word remains true in the saying, it is, give up everything for the sake of the Lord. This is a hard and long task, but you can begin it here and now. Bit by bit we must go towards it.

The goal of man is to go beyond law. And enjoyment can never be the goal, because enjoyment can only be in nature. Alas, alas, the desire for enjoyment does not leave a man.

Enjoyment, misery, luxury, wealth, power, and poverty, even life itself, are all evanescent.

Everything that has selfishness for its basis, competition as its right hand, and enjoyment as its goal, must die sooner or later. Such things must die.

Enjoyment is the million-headed serpent that we must tread under foot. We renounce and go on, then find nothing and despair; but hold on, hold on . The world is a demon. It is a kingdom of which the puny ego is king.

Put it away and stand firm. Give up lust and gold and fame and hold fast to the Lord, and at last we shall reach a state of perfect indifference. The idea that the gratification of the senses constitutes enjoyment is purely materialistic. There is not one spark of real enjoyment there; all the joy there is, is a mere reflection of the true bliss.

Plunder and fight as you may, the enjoyment that you are seeking is only in peace; and peace, in the renunciation of physical pleasures. Enjoyment lies not in physical development, but in the culture of the mind and the intellect.

Is enjoyment the goal of life? Were it so, it would be a tremendous mistake to become a man at all. What man can enjoy a meal with more gusto than the dog or the cat ? Go to a menagerie and see the [wild animals] tearing the flesh from the bone. Go back and become a bird! What a mistake then to become a man! Vain have been my years — hundreds of years — of struggle only to become the man of sense-enjoyments.

What is the goal of it all? Can senses ever be the goal? Can enjoyment of pleasure ever be the goal? Can this life ever be the goal of the soul? If it is, better die this moment; do not want this life! If that is the fate of man, that he is going to be only the perfected machine, it would just mean that we go back to being trees and stones and things like that.

Did you ever hear a cow tell a lie or see a tree steal? They are perfect machines. They do not make mistakes. They live in a world where everything is finished.

So long as enjoyment is sought, bondage remains. Only imperfection can enjoy, because enjoyment is the fulfilling of desire. The human soul enjoys nature. The underlying reality of nature, soul, and God is Brahman; but It (Brahman) is unseen, until we bring It out.

It may be brought out by Pramantha or friction, just as we can produce fire by friction. The body is the lower piece of wood, Om is the pointed piece and Dhyâna (meditation) is the friction. When this is used, that light which is the knowledge of Brahman will burst forth in the soul.

The lower the animal, the more is its enjoyment in the senses, the more it lives in the senses. Civilisation, true civilization, should mean the power of taking the animal-man out of his sense-life — by giving him visions and tastes of planes much higher — and not external comforts.

Man knows this instinctively. He may not formulate it to himself under all circumstances. He may form very divergent opinions about the life of thought. But it is there, pressing itself to the front in spite of everything, making him pay reverence to the hoodoo-worker, the medicine-man, the magician, the priest, or the professor of science.

The growth of man can only be gauged by his power of living in the higher atmosphere where the senses are left behind, the amount of the pure thought-oxygen his lungs can breathe in, and the amount of time he can spend on that height.

As it is, it is an obvious fact that, with the exception of what is taken up by the necessities of life, the man of culture is loth to spend his time on so-called comforts, and even necessary actions are performed with lessened zeal, as the process moves forward.

The other great mistake we often make is that good is taken as an ever-increasing item, whilst evil is a fixed quantity. From this it is argued that evil being diminished every day, there will come a time when good alone will remain.

The fallacy lies in the assumption of a false premise. If good is increasing, so is evil. My desires have been much more than the desires of the masses among my race. My joys have been much greater than theirs — but my miseries a million times more intense. The same constitution that makes you feel the least touch of good makes you feel the least of evil too. The same nerves that carry sensations of pleasure carry the sensations of pain too — and the same mind feels both.

The progress of the world means more enjoyment and more misery too. This mixture of life and death, good and evil, knowledge and ignorance is what is called Maya — or the universal phenomenon.

You may go on for eternity inside this net, seeking for happiness — you find much, and much evil too. To have good and no evil is childish nonsense.

Two ways are left open — one by giving up all hope to take up the world as it is and bear the pangs and pains in the hope of a crumb of happiness now and then. The other, to give up the search for pleasure, knowing it to be pain in another form, and seek for truth — and those that dare try for truth succeed in finding that truth as ever present — present in themselves.

Then we also discover how the same truth is manifesting itself both in our relative error and knowledge — we find also that the same truth is bliss which again is manifesting itself as good and evil, and with it also we find real existence which is manifesting itself as both death and life.

Nowadays people among the backward nations, and among the less cultured portion of the civilised people of the West are laying much stress on the non-essential. Among the cultured and the wealthy, matters are on a different footing. The wealthy are either immersed in the enjoyment of health or grubbing for more. They, and a large section of the busy people, say of religion that it is rot, stuff, nonsense, and they honestly think so.

There never was a person who found happiness in the senses or in enjoyment of the senses. The world is our fish basket, we must not depend upon it for enjoyment. This is a place for action, not enjoyment.

Through enjoyment Yoga will come in time. But alas, such is the lot of my countrymen that, not to speak of possessing yoga, they cannot even have a little Bhoga! Suffering all sorts of indignities they can with the utmost difficulty only meet the barest needs of the body—and even that everyone cannot do! It is strange that such a state of affairs does not disturb our sleep and rouse us to our immediate duties.

To the vast majority of mankind, the body is everything; the body is all the universe to them; bodily enjoyment is their all in all. This demon of the worship of the body and of the things of the body has entered into us all. We may indulge in tall talk and take very high flights, but we are like vultures all the same; our mind is directed to the piece of carrion down below.

Why should our body be saved, say, from the tiger? Why may we not give it over to the tiger? The tiger will thereby be pleased, and that is not altogether so very far from self-sacrifice and worship.

Can you reach the realization of such an idea in which all sense of self is completely lost? It is a very dizzy height on the pinnacle of the religion of love, and few in this world have ever climbed up to it; but until a man reaches that highest point of ever-ready and ever-willing self-sacrifice, he cannot become a perfect Bhakta.

We may all manage to maintain our bodies more or less satisfactorily and for longer or shorter intervals of time. Nevertheless, our bodies have to go; there is no permanence about them. Blessed are they whose bodies get destroyed in the service of others.

"Wealth, and even life itself, the sage always holds ready for the service of others. In this world, there being one thing certain, viz death, it is far better that this body dies in a good cause than in a bad one."

We may drag our life on for fifty years or a hundred years; but after that, what is it that happens? Everything that is the result of combination must get dissolved and die. There must and will come a time for it to be decomposed. Jesus and Buddha and Mohammed are all dead; all the great Prophets and Teachers of the world are dead.

The history of the world shows that evil is a continuously increasing quantity, as well as good. Take the lowest man; he lives in the forest. His sense of enjoyment is very small, and so also is his power to suffer.

His misery is entirely on the sense-plane. If he does not get plenty of food, he is miserable; but give him plenty of food and freedom to rove and to hunt, and he is perfectly happy. His happiness consists only in the senses, and so does his misery also.

But if that man increases in knowledge, his happiness will increase, the intellect will open to him, and his sense-enjoyment will evolve into intellectual enjoyment. He will feel pleasure in reading a beautiful poem, and a mathematical problem will be of absorbing interest to him. But, with these, the inner nerves will become more and more susceptible to miseries of mental pain, of which the savage does not think.

Take a very simple illustration. In Tibet there is no marriage, and there is no jealousy, yet we know that marriage is a much higher state. The Tibetans have not known the wonderful enjoyment, the blessing of chastity, the happiness of having a chaste, virtuous wife, or a chaste, virtuous husband. These people cannot feel that.

And similarly they do not feel the intense jealousy of the chaste wife or husband, or the misery caused by unfaithfulness on either side, with all the heart-burnings and sorrows which believers in chastity experience. On one side, the latter gain happiness, but on the other, they suffer misery too.

Work

Be perfectly resigned, perfectly unconcerned; then alone can you do any true work. No eyes can see the real forces; we can only see the results. Put out self, forget it; just let God work, it is His business.

By work alone men may get to where Buddha got largely by meditation or Christ by prayer. Buddha was a working Jnâni, Christ was a Bhakta, but the same goal was reached by both of them.

Do any deserve liberty who are not ready to give it to others? Let us calmly go to work, instead of dissipating our energy in unnecessary fretting and fuming.

Each work has to pass through these stages—ridicule, opposition, and then acceptance. Those who think ahead of their time are sure to be misunderstood.

Even the greatest fool can accomplish a task if it were after his or her heart. But the intelligent ones are those who can convert every work into one that suits their taste.

No work is petty. Everything in this world is like a banyan-seed, which, though appearing tiny as a mustard-seed, has yet the gigantic banyan tree latent within it. He indeed is intelligent who notices this and succeeds in making all work truly great.

Every man who, we think, gets something by chance, has been working for it slowly and surely through ages.

In a truly noble work, not to speak of men, even God Himself befriends the doer.

It is a good discipline to be forced to work for work's sake, even to the length of not being allowed to enjoy the fruits of one's labour.

No foolish talk now, but actual work.

Not a work will be lost, no struggle vain. . .

On and on, work, work, work.

Our great defect in life is that we are so much drawn to the ideal, the goal is so much more enchanting, so much more alluring, so much bigger in our mental horizon, that we lose sight of the details altogether… One of the greatest lessons I have learnt in my life is to pay as much attention to the means of work as to its end. He was a great man from whom I learnt it, and his own life was a practical demonstration of this great principle I have been always learning great lessons from that one principle, and it appears to me that all the secret of success is there; to pay as much attention to the means as to the end.

The man who says that he will work when the world has become all good and then he will enjoy bliss is as likely to succeed as the man who sits beside the Ganga and says, "I will ford the river when all the water has run into the ocean."

The result of every work is mixed with good and evil. There is no good work that has not a touch of evil in it. Like smoke round the fire, some evil always clings to work. We should engage in such works as bring the largest amount of good and the smallest measure of evil.

The sun = Knowledge. The stormy water = Work. The lotus = Love. The serpent = Yoga. The swan = the Self. The Motto = May the Swan (the Supreme Self) send us that. It is the mind-lake. (Swami Vivekananda's explanation of Ramakrishna Mission's emblem)

There are certain works which are, as it were, the aggregate, the sum total, of a large number of smaller works. If we stand near the seashore and hear the waves dashing against the shingle, we think it is such a great noise, and yet we know that one wave is really composed of millions and millions of minute waves. Each one of these is making a noise, and yet we do not catch it; it is only when they become the big aggregate that we hear. Similarly, every pulsation of the heart is work. Certain kinds of work we feel and they become tangible to us; they are, at the same time, the aggregate of a number of small works. If you really want to judge of the character of a man, look not at his great performances. Every fool may become a hero at one time or another. Watch a man do his most common actions; those are indeed the things which will tell you the real character of a great man. Great occasions rouse even the lowest of human beings to some kind of greatness, but he alone is the really great man whose character is great always, the same wherever he be.

This world is not for cowards. Do not try to fly. Look not for success or failure. Join yourself to the perfectly unselfish will and work on. Know that the mind which is born to succeed joins itself to a determined will and perseveres. You have the right to work, but do not become so degenerate as to look for results. Work incessantly, but see something behind the work. Even good deeds can find a man in great bondage. Therefore be not bound by good deeds or by desire for name and fame. Those who know this secret pass beyond this round of birth and death and become immortal.

To attain liberation through work, join yourself to work but without desire, looking for no result. Such work leads to knowledge, which in turn brings emancipation. To give up work before you know, leads to misery. Work done for the Self gives no bondage. Neither desire pleasure nor fear pain from work. It is the mind and body that work, not I. Tell yourself this unceasingly and realise it. Try not to know that you work.

To work properly… you have first to give up the idea of attachment. Secondly, do not mix in the fray, hold yourself as a witness and go on working. My master used to say, "Look upon your children as a nurse does." The nurse will take your baby and fondle it and play with it and behave towards it as gently as if it were her own child; but as soon as you give her notice to quit, she is ready to start off bag and baggage from the house. Everything in the shape of attachment is forgotten.

We also read this in the Gita and learn that we have to work, constantly work with all our power; to put our whole mind in the work, whatever it be, that we are doing. At the same time, we must not be attached. That is to say, we must not be drawn away from the work by anything else; still, we must be able to quit the work whenever we like.

We read in the Bhagavad-Gita again and again that we must all work incessantly. All work is by nature composed of good and evil. We cannot do any work which will not do some good somewhere; there cannot be any work which will not cause some harm somewhere. Every work must necessarily be a mixture of good and evil; yet we are commanded to work incessantly. Good and evil will both have their results, will produce their Karma. Good action will entail upon us good effect; bad action, bad. But good and bad are both bondages of the soul. The solution reached in the Gita in regard to this bondage-producing nature of work is that, if we do not attach ourselves to the work we do, it will not have any binding effect on our soul. We shall try to understand what is meant by this "non-attachment to" to work.

When you are doing any work, do not think of anything beyond. Do it as worship.

Work and worship are necessary to take away the veil, to lift off the bondage and illusion.

Work for the idea, not the person.

Work incessantly, but be not attached to it.

Work on, brave hearts, fail not — no saying nay; work on — the Lord is behind the work. Mahâshakti is with you.

Work on! Hold on! Be brave! Dare anything and everything!

Work on, my brave boys. We shall see the light some day. Let things slowly grow. Rome was not built in a day.

Work on with a heart.

Work on with energy.

Work on with the intrepidity of a lion but, at the same time with the tenderness of a flower.

Work out the salvation of this land and of the whole world, each of you thinking that the entire burden is on your shoulders.

Work through freedom! Work through love! The word "love" is very difficult to understand; love never comes until there is freedom. There is no true love possible in the slave.

Work unto death — I am with you, and when I am gone, my spirit will work with you.

Work, work — conquer all by your love!

Work, work, for, to work only for the good of others is life.

Work, work the idea, the plan, my boys, my brave, noble, good souls — to the wheel, to the wheel put your shoulders!

Work, work, work — let this be your motto.

Listen to an old story. A lazy tramp sauntering along the road saw an old man sitting at the door of his house and stopped to inquire of him the whereabouts of a certain place. "How far is such and such a village?" he asked. The old man remained silent. The man repeated his query several times. Still there was no answer. Disgusted at this, the traveller turned to go away. The old man then stood up and said, "The village of — is only a mile from here." "What!" said the tramp, "Why did you not speak when I asked you before?" "Because then", said the old man, "you seemed so halting and careless about proceeding, but now you are starting off in good earnest, and you have a right to an answer."

Will you remember this story, my son? Go to work, the rest will come: "Whosoever not trusting in anything else but Me, rests on Me, I supply him with everything he needs" (Gitâ, IX. 22). This is no dream.

Even the lowest forms of work are not to be despised. Let the man, who knows no better, work for selfish ends, for name and fame; but everyone should always try to get towards higher and higher motives and to understand them. "To work we have the right, but not to the fruits thereof:" Leave the fruits alone. Why care for results? If you wish to help a man, never think what that man's attitude should be towards you. If you want to do a great or a good work, do not trouble to think what the result will be.

What Is Duty

The ordinary idea of duty everywhere is that every good man follows the dictates of his conscience. But what is it that makes an act a duty?

If a Christian finds a piece of beef before him and does not eat it to save his own life, or will not give it to save the life of another man, he is sure to feel that he has not done his duty. But if a Hindu dares to eat that piece of beef or to give it to another Hindu, he is equally sure to feel that he too has not done his duty; the Hindu's training and education make him feel that way.

In the last century there were notorious bands of robbers in India called thugs; they thought it their duty to kill any man they could and take away his money; the larger the number of men they killed, the better they thought they were.

Ordinarily if a man goes out into the street and shoots down another man, he is apt to feel sorry for it, thinking that he has done wrong. But if the very same man, as a soldier in his regiment, kills not one but twenty, he is certain to feel glad and think that he has done his duty remarkably well.

Therefore we see that it is not the thing done that defines a duty. To give an objective definition of duty is thus entirely impossible.

Yet there is duty from the subjective side. Any action that makes us go Godward is a good action, and is our duty; any action that makes us go downward is evil, and is not our duty.

From the subjective standpoint we may see that certain acts have a tendency to exalt and ennoble us, while certain other acts have a tendency to degrade and to brutalise us. But it is not possible to make out with certainty which acts have which kind of tendency in relation to all persons, of all sorts and conditions.

There is, however, only one idea of duty which has been universally accepted by all mankind, of all ages and sects and countries, and that has been summed up in a Sanskrit aphorism thus: "Do not injure any being; not injuring any being is virtue, injuring any being is sin."

The idea of duty varies much among different nations. In one country, if a man does not do certain things, people will say he has acted wrongly; while if he does those very things in another country, people will say that he did not act rightly — and yet we know that there must be some universal idea of duty. In the same way, one class of society thinks that certain things are among its duty, while another class thinks quite the opposite and would be horrified if it had to do those things.

Two ways are left open to us — the way of the ignorant, who think that there is only one way to truth and that all the rest are wrong, and the way of the wise, who admit that, according to our mental constitution or the different planes of existence in which we are, duty and morality may vary.

The important thing is to know that there are gradations of duty and of morality — that the duty of one state of life, in one set of circumstances, will not and cannot be that of another.

The Bhagavad-Gita frequently alludes to duties dependent upon birth and position in life. Birth and position in life and in society largely determine the mental and moral attitude of individuals towards the various activities of life. It is therefore our duty to do that work which will exalt and ennoble us in accordance with the ideals and activities of the society in which we are born.

But it must be particularly remembered that the same ideals and activities do not prevail in all societies and countries; our ignorance of this is the main cause of much of the hatred of one nation towards another. An American thinks that whatever an American does in accordance with the custom of his country is the best thing to do, and that whoever does not follow his custom must be a very wicked man. A Hindu thinks that his customs are the only right ones and are the best in the world, and that whosoever does not obey them must be the most wicked man living.

This is quite a natural mistake which all of us are apt to make. But it is very harmful; it is the cause of half the uncharitableness found in the world.

When I came to this country and was going through the Chicago Fair, a man from behind pulled at my turban. I looked back and saw that he was a very gentlemanly-looking man, neatly dressed. I spoke to him; and when he found that I knew English, he became very much abashed.

On another occasion in the same Fair another man gave me a push. When I asked him the reason, he also was ashamed and stammered out an apology saying, "Why do you dress that way?"

The sympathies of these men were limited within the range of their own language and their own fashion of dress. Much of the oppression of powerful nations on weaker ones is caused by this prejudice. It dries up their fellow feeling for fellow men.

That very man who asked me why I did not dress as he did and wanted to ill-treat me because of my dress may have been a very good man, a good father, and a good citizen; but the kindliness of his nature died out as soon as he saw a man in a different dress. Strangers are exploited in all countries, because they do not know how to defend themselves; thus they carry home false impressions of the peoples they have seen.

Sailors, soldiers, and traders behave in foreign lands in very queer ways, although they would not dream of doing so in their own country; perhaps this is why the Chinese call Europeans and Americans "foreign devils". They could not have done this if they had met the good, the kindly sides of Western life.

We should always try to see the duty of others through their own eyes, and never judge the customs of other peoples by our own standard. I am not the standard of the universe. I have to accommodate myself to the world, and not the world to me. So we see that environments change the nature of our duties, and doing the duty which is ours at any particular time is the best thing we can do in this world. Let us do that duty which is ours by birth; and when we have done that, let us do the duty which is ours by our position in life and in society.

There is, however, one great danger in human nature, viz that man never examines himself. He thinks he is quite as fit to be on the throne as the king. Even if he is, he must first show that he has done the duty of his own position; and then higher duties will come to him. When we begin to work earnestly in the world, nature gives us blows right and left and soon enables us to find out our position.

No man can long occupy satisfactorily a position for which he is not fit. There is no use in grumbling against nature's adjustment. He who does the lower work is not therefore a lower man. No man is to be judged by the mere nature of his duties, but all should be judged by the manner and the spirit in which they perform them.

Later on we shall find that even this idea of duty undergoes change, and that the greatest work is done only when there is no selfish motive to prompt it. Yet it is work through the sense of duty that leads us to work without any idea of duty; when work will become worship — nay, something higher — then will work be done for its own sake.

We shall find that the philosophy of duty, whether it be in the form of ethics or of love, is the same as in every other Yoga — the object being the attenuating of the lower self, so that the real higher Self may shine forth — the lessening of the frittering away of energies on the lower plane of existence, so that the soul may manifest itself on the higher ones. This is accomplished by the continuous denial of low desires, which duty rigorously requires.

The whole organisation of society has thus been developed, consciously or unconsciously, in the realms of action and experience, where, by limiting selfishness, we open the way to an unlimited expansion of the real nature of man.

Devotion To Duty

Each duty has its own place, and according to the circumstances in which we are placed, we must perform our duties. what is duty for one is not duty for another. At the same time, we do not say that this duty is lowering and the other elevating.

Isolation of the soul from all objects, mental and physical, is the goal; when that is attained, the soul will find that it was alone all the time, and it required no one to make it happy. As long as we require someone else to make us happy, we are slaves. When the Purusha finds that It is free, and does not require anything to complete Itself, that this nature is quite unnecessary, then freedom (Kaivalya) is attained.

Men run after a few dollars and do not think anything of cheating a fellow-being to get those dollars; but if they would restrain themselves, in a few years they would develop such characters as would bring them millions of dollars — if they wanted them. Then their will would govern the universe. But we are all such fools!

What is the use of talking of one's mistakes to the world? They cannot thereby be undone. For what one has done one must suffer; one must try and do better. The world sympathises only with the strong and the powerful.

It is only work that is done as a free-will offering to humanity and to nature that does not bring with it any binding attachment.

Duty of any kind is not to be slighted. A man who does the lower work is not, for that reason only, a lower man than he who does the higher work; a man should not be judged by the nature of his duties, but by the manner in which he does them. His manner of doing them and his power to do them are indeed the test of a man. A shoemaker who can turn out a strong, nice pair of shoes in the shortest possible time is a better man, according to his profession and his work, than a professor who talks nonsense every day of his life.

Every duty is holy, and devotion to duty is the highest form of the worship of God; it is certainly a source of great help in enlightening and emancipating the deluded and ignorance-encumbered souls of the Baddhas — the bound ones.

By doing well the duty which is nearest to us, the duty which is in our hands now, we make ourselves stronger and improving our strength in this manner step by step, we may even reach a state in which it shall be our privilege to do the most coveted and honoured duties in life and in society.

Our first duty is not to hate ourselves, because to advance we must have faith in ourselves first and then in God. He who has no faith in himself can never have faith in God. Therefore, the only alternative remaining to us is to recognise that duty and morality vary under different circumstances; not that the man who resists evil is doing what is always and in itself wrong, but that in the different circumstances in which he is placed it may become even his duty to resist evil.

All great teachers have taught, "Resist not evil," that non-resistance is the highest moral ideal. We all know that, if a certain number of us attempted to put that maxim fully into practice, the whole social fabric would fall to pieces, the wicked would take possession of our properties and our lives, and would do whatever they liked with us. Even if only one day of such non-resistance were practiced, it would lead to disaster.

Yet, intuitively, in our heart of hearts we feel the truth of the teaching "Resist not evil." This seems to us to be the highest ideal; yet to teach this doctrine only would be equivalent to condemning a vast portion of mankind.

Not only so, it would be making men feel that they were always doing wrong, and cause in them scruples of conscience in all their actions; it would weaken them, and that constant self-disapproval would breed more vice than any other weakness would. To the man who has begun to hate himself the gate to degeneration has already opened; and the same is true of a nation.

He who has no faith in himself can never have faith in God. Therefore, the only alternative remaining to us is to recognise that duty and morality vary under different circumstances; not that the man who resists evil is doing what is always and in itself wrong, but that in the different circumstances in which he is placed it may become even his duty to resist evil.

You should cultivate a noble nature by doing your duty. By doing our duty we get rid of the idea of duty; and then and then only we feel everything as done by God. We are but machines in His hand. This body is opaque, God is the lamp. Whatever is going out of the body is God's.

You do not feel it. You feel "I". This is delusion. You must learn calm submission to the will of God. Duty is the best school for it. This duty is morality.

Drill yourself to be thoroughly submissive. Get rid of the "I". No humbuggism. Then you can get rid of the idea of duty; for all is His. Then you go on naturally, forgiving, forgetting, etc.

Our religion always presents different gradations of duty and religion to different people.

Duty is seldom sweet. It is only when love greases its wheels that it runs smoothly; it is a continuous friction otherwise.

How else could parents do their duties to their children, husbands to their wives, and vice versa? Do we not meet with cases of friction every day in our lives? Duty is sweet only through love, and love shines in freedom alone.

Yet is it freedom to be a slave to the senses, to anger, to jealousies and a hundred other petty things that must occur every day in human life? In all these little roughnesses that we meet with in life, the highest expression of freedom is to forbear.

Women, slaves to their own irritable, jealous tempers, are apt to blame their husbands, and assert their own "freedom", as they think, not knowing that thereby they only prove that they are slaves. So it is with husbands who eternally find fault with their wives.

There is a sage in India, a great Yogi, one of the most wonderful men I have ever seen in my life. He is a peculiar man, he will not teach any one; if you ask him a question he will not answer. It is too much for him to take up the position of a teacher, he will not do it. If you ask a question, and wait for some days, in the course of conversation he will bring up the subject, and wonderful light will he throw on it.

He told me once the secret of work, "Let the end and the means be joined into one." When you are doing any work, do not think of anything beyond. Do it as worship, as the highest worship, and devote your whole life to it for the time being.

Thus, in the story, the Vyadha and the woman did their duty with cheerfulness and whole-heartedness; and the result was that they became illuminated, clearly showing that the right performance of the duties of any station in life, without attachment to results, leads us to the highest realisation of the perfection of the soul.

It is the worker who is attached to results that grumbles about the nature of the duty which has fallen to his lot. To the unattached worker all duties are equally good, and form efficient instruments with which selfishness and sensuality may be killed, and the freedom of the soul secured.

We are all apt to think too highly of ourselves. Our duties are determined by our desires to a much larger extent than we are willing to grant. Competition rouses envy, and it kills the kindliness of the heart. To the grumbler all duties are distasteful; nothing will ever satisfy him, and his whole life is doomed to prove a failure.

Let us work on, doing as we go whatever happens to be our duty, and being ever ready to put our shoulders to the wheel. Then surely shall we see the Light!

Karma-Yoga teaches us that the ordinary idea of duty is on the lower plane; nevertheless, all of us have to do our duty. Yet we may see that this peculiar sense of duty is very often a great cause of misery.

Duty becomes a disease with us; it drags us ever forward. It catches hold of us and makes our whole life miserable. It is the bane of human life. This duty, this idea of duty is the midday summer sun which scorches the innermost soul of mankind.

Look at those poor slaves to duty! Duty leaves them no time to say prayers, no time to bathe. Duty is ever on them. They go out and work. Duty is on them!

They come home and think of the work for the next day. Duty is on them! It is living a slave's life, at last dropping down in the street and dying in harness, like a horse.

This is duty as it is understood.

What is duty after all? It is really the impulsion of the flesh, of our attachment; and when an attachment has become established, we call it duty.

It is, so to say, a sort of chronic disease. When it is acute, we call it disease; when it is chronic, we call it nature. It is a disease.

So when attachment becomes chronic, we baptise it with the high sounding name of duty. We strew flowers upon it, trumpets sound for it, sacred texts are said over it, and then the whole world fights, and men earnestly rob each other for this duty's sake.

Duty is good to the extent that it checks brutality. To the lowest kinds of men, who cannot have any other ideal, it is of some good; but those who want to be Karma-Yogis must throw this idea of duty overboard. There is no duty for you and me. Whatever you have to give to the world, do give by all means, but not as a duty. Do not take any thought of that. Be not compelled.

Unity in variety is the plan of creation. However men and women may vary individually, there is unity in the background. The different individual characters and classes of men and women are natural variations in creation.

Hence, we ought not to judge them by the same standard or put the same ideal before them. Such a course creates only an unnatural struggle, and the result is that man begins to hate himself and is hindered from becoming religious and good. Our duty is to encourage every one in his struggle to live up to his own highest ideal, and strive at the same time to make the ideal as near as possible to the truth.

In the material physical world, expansion is life, and contraction is death. Whatever ceases to expand ceases to live. Translating this in the moral world we have: If one would expand, he must love, and when he ceases to love he dies. It is your nature; you must, because that is the only law of life.

Therefore, we must love God for love's sake, so we must do our duty for duty's sake; we must work for work's sake without looking for any reward — know that you are purer and more perfect, know that this is the real temple of God.

Every man should take up his own ideal and endeavour to accomplish it. That is a surer way of progress than taking up other men's ideals, which he can never hope to accomplish.

For instance, we take a child and at once give him the task of walking twenty miles. Either the little one dies, or one in a thousand crawls the twenty miles, to reach the end exhausted and half-dead.

That is like what we generally try to do with the world. All the men and women, in any society, are not of the same mind, capacity, or of the same power to do things; they must have different ideals, and we have no right to sneer at any ideal. Let everyone do the best he can for realising his own ideal.

Nor is it right that I should be judged by your standard or you by mine. The apple tree should not be judged by the standard of the oak, nor the oak by that of the apple. To judge the apple tree you must take the apple standard, and for the oak, its own standard.

Selfishness

Keeping aloof from the community of nations is the only cause for the downfall of India. Since the English came, they have been forcing you back into communion with other nations, and you are visibly rising again. Everyone that comes out of the country confers a benefit on the whole nation; for it is by doing that alone that your horizon will expand. And as women cannot avail themselves of this advantage, they have made almost no progress in India. There is no station of rest; either you progress upwards or you go back and die out. The only sign of life is going outward and forward and expansion. Contraction is death. Why should you do good to others? Because that is the only condition of life; thereby you expand beyond your little self; you live and grow. All narrowness, all contraction, all selfishness is simply slow suicide, and when a nation commits the fatal mistake of contracting itself and of thus cutting off all expansion and life, it must die. Women similarly must go forward or become idiots and soulless tools in the hands of their tyrannical lords. The children are the result of the combination of the tyrant and the idiot, and they are slaves . And this is the whole history of modern India. Oh, who would break this horrible crystallisation of death? Lord help us!

Beware! All expansion is life, all contraction is death. All love is expansions all selfishness is contraction. Love is therefore the only law of life. He who loves lives, he who is selfish is dying. Therefore love for love's sake, because it is the only law of life, just as you breathe to live. This is the secret of selfless love, selfless action and the rest.

Even misery can be enjoyed when there is no selfishness, when we have become the witness of our own lives.

It is selfishness that we must seek to eliminate. I find that whenever I have made a mistake in my life, it has always been because self entered into the calculation. Where self has not been involved, my judgment has gone straight to the mark.

Without self, there would have been no religious system. If man had not wanted anything for himself, do you think he would have had all this praying and worship? Why! he would never have thought of God at all, except perhaps for a little praise now and then, at the sight of a beautiful landscape or something. And that is the only attitude there ought to be. All praise and thanks. If only we were rid of self!

In this evanescent world, where everything is falling to pieces, we have to make the highest use of what time we have. It is the horrible body-idea that breeds all the selfishness in the world, just this one delusion that we are wholly the body we own, and that we must by all possible means try our very best to preserve and to please it. If you know that you are positively other than your body, you have then none to fight with or struggle against; you are dead to all ideas of selfishness. So the Bhakta declares that we have to hold ourselves as if we are altogether dead to all the things of the world; and that is indeed self-surrender. Let things come as they may. This is the meaning of "Thy will be done" — not going about fighting and struggling and thinking all the while that God wills all our own weaknesses and worldly ambitions. It may be that good comes even out of our selfish struggles; that is, however, God's look-out. The perfected Bhakta's idea must be never to will and work for himself.

It is the same story all over the country. But then, it is not as a result of pure wickedness that the selfishness commonly met with in our country has come. This bestial selfishness is the outcome of centuries of failure and repression. It is not real selfishness, but deep-rooted despair. It will be cored at the first inkling of success.

Selfishness is the chief sin, thinking of ourselves first. He who thinks, "I will eat first, I will have more money than others, and I will possess everything", he who thinks, "I will get to heaven before others I will get Mukti before others" is the selfish man. The unselfish man says, "I will be last, I do not care to go to heaven, I will even go to hell if by doing so I can help my brothers." This unselfishness is the test of religion. He who has more of this unselfishness is more spiritual and nearer to Shiva. Whether he is learned or ignorant, he is nearer to Shiva than anybody else, whether he knows it or not. And if a man is selfish, even though he has visited all the temples, seen all the places of pilgrimage, and painted himself like a leopard, he is still further off from Shiva.

Selfishness is the devil incarnate in every man. Every bit of self, bit by bit, is devil. Take off self by one side and God enters by the other. When the self is got rid of, only God remains. Light and darkness cannot remain together.

The cause of evil is our desire to be superior to others and our selfishness.

The practical side of Vedanta morality is necessary as much today as it ever was, more necessary, perhaps, than it ever was, for all this privilege-claiming has become tremendously intensified with the extension of knowledge. The idea of God and the devil, or Ahura Mazda and Ahriman, has a good deal of poetry in it. The difference between God and the devil is in nothing except in unselfishness and selfishness. The devil knows as much as God, is as powerful as God; only he has no holiness — that makes him a devil. Apply the same idea to the modern world: excess of knowledge and power, without holiness, makes human beings devils.

This was the basis of his (Gautama Buddha) religion. So long as society tries to cure human selfishness by laws and institutions whose aim is to force others to do good to their neighbors, nothing can be done. The remedy is not to place trick against trick and force against force. The only remedy is in making unselfish men and women. You may enact laws to cure present evils, but they will be of no avail.

We must do the work and find out the motive power that prompts us; and, almost without exception, in the first years, we shall find that our motives are always selfish; but gradually this selfishness will melt by persistence, till at last will come the time when we shall be able to do really unselfish work. We may all hope that some day or other, as we struggle through the paths of life, there will come a time when we shall become perfectly unselfish; and the moment we attain to that, all our powers will be concentrated, and the knowledge which is ours will be manifest.

Get up, and put your shoulders to the wheel — how long is this life for? As you have come into this world, leave some mark behind. Otherwise, where is the difference between you and the trees and stones? They, too, come into existence, decay and die. If you like to be born and to die like them, you are at liberty to do so. Show me by your actions that your reading the Vedanta has been fruitful of the highest good. Go and tell all, "In every one of you lies that Eternal Power", and try to wake It up. What will you do with individual salvation? That is sheer selfishness. Throw aside your meditation, throw away your salvation and such things! Put your whole heart and soul in the work to which I have consecrated myself.

Work and Unattachment

This whole universe is only one speck of the infinite being; and all our laws, our bondages, our joys and our sorrows, our happinesses and our expectations, are only within this small universe; all our progression and digression are within its small compass.

So you see how childish it is to expect a continuation of this universe — the creation of our minds — and to expect to go to heaven, which after all must mean only a repetition of this world that we know. You see at once that it is an impossible and childish desire to make the whole of infinite existence conform to the limited and conditioned existence which we know.

When a man says that he will have again and again this same thing which he is hating now, or, as I sometimes put it, when he asks for a comfortable religion, you may know that he has become so degenerate that he cannot think of anything higher than what he is now; he is just his little present surroundings and nothing more. He has forgotten his infinite nature, and his whole idea is confined to these little joys, and sorrows, and heart-jealousies of the moment.

He thinks that this finite thing is the infinite; and not only so, he will not let this foolishness go. He clings on desperately unto Trishnâ, and the thirst after life, what the Buddhists call Tanhâ and Tissâ. There may be millions of kinds of happiness, and beings, and laws, and progress, and causation, all acting outside the little universe that we know; and, after all, the whole of this comprises but one section of our infinite nature.

To acquire freedom we have to get beyond the limitations of this universe; it cannot be found here. Perfect equilibrium, or what the Christians call the peace that passeth all understanding, cannot be had in this universe, nor in heaven, nor in any place where our mind and thoughts can go, where the senses can feel, or which the imagination can conceive.

No such place can give us that freedom, because all such places would be within our universe, and it is limited by space, time, and causation. There may be places that are more ethereal than this earth of ours, where enjoyments may be keener, but even those places must be in the universe and, therefore, in bondage to law; so we have to go beyond, and real religion begins where this little universe ends. These little joys, and sorrows, and knowledge of things end there, and the reality begins.

Until we give up the thirst after life, the strong attachment to this our transient conditioned existence we have no hope of catching even a glimpse of that infinite freedom beyond. It stands to reason then that there is only one way to attain to that freedom which is the goal of all the noblest aspirations of mankind, and that is by giving up this little life, giving up this little universe, giving up this earth, giving up heaven, giving up the body, giving up the mind, giving up everything that is limited and conditioned.

If we give up our attachment to this little universe of the senses or of the mind, we shall be free immediately. The only way to come out of bondage is to go beyond the limitations of law, to go beyond causation.

But it is a most difficult thing to give up the clinging to this universe; few ever attain to that. There are two ways to do that mentioned in our books. One is called the "Neti, Neti" (not this, not this), the other is called "Iti" (this); the former is the negative, and the latter is the positive way.

The negative way is the most difficult. It is only possible to the men of the very highest, exceptional minds and gigantic wills who simply stand up and say, "No, I will not have this," and the mind and body obey their will, and they come out successful.

But such people are very rare. The vast majority of mankind choose the positive way, the way through the world, making use of all the bondages themselves to break those very bondages. This is also a kind of giving up; only it is done slowly and gradually, by knowing things, enjoying things and thus obtaining experience, and knowing the nature of things until the mind lets them all go at last and becomes unattached.

The former way of obtaining non-attachment is by reasoning, and the latter way is through work and experience. The first is the path of Jnâna-Yoga, and is characterized by the refusal to do any work; the second is that of Karma-Yoga, in which there is no cessation from work.

Every one must work in the universe. Only those who are perfectly satisfied with the Self, whose desires do not go beyond the Self, whose mind never strays out of the Self, to whom the Self is all in all, only those do not work. The rest must work.

A current rushing down of its own nature falls into a hollow and makes a whirlpool, and, after running a little in that whirlpool, it emerges again in the form of the free current to go on unchecked. Each human life is like that current. It gets into the whirl, gets involved in this world of space, time, and causation, whirls round a little, crying out, "my father, my brother, my name, my fame", and so on, and at last emerges out of it and regains its original freedom.

The whole universe is doing that. Whether we know it or not, whether we are conscious or unconscious of it, we are all working to get out of the dream of the world. Man's experience in the world is to enable him to get out of its whirlpool.

As children we all think that the world is made so very nice, and that masses of pleasures are simply waiting for our going out to them. That is every schoolboy's dream. And when he goes out into the world, the everyday world, very soon his dreams vanish. So with nations. When they see how every city is built upon ruins — every forest stands upon a city — then they become convinced of the vanity of this world.

All the power of knowledge and wealth once made has passed away — all the sciences of the ancients, lost, lost forever. Nobody knows how. That teaches us a grand lesson. Vanity of vanities; all is vanity and vexation of the spirit. If we have seen all this, then we become disgusted with this world and all it offers us. This is called Vairâgya, non-attachment, and is the first step towards knowledge.

To attain this unattachment is almost a life-work, but as soon as we have reached this point, we have attained the goal of love and become free; the bondage of nature falls from us, and we see nature as she is; she forges no more chains for us; we stand entirely free and take not the results of work into consideration; who then cares for what the results may be?

Do you ask anything from your children in return for what you have given them? It is your duty to work for them, and there the matter ends. In whatever you do for a particular person, a city, or a state, assume the same attitude towards it as you have towards your children — expect nothing in return. If you can invariably take the position of a giver, in which everything given by you is a free offering to the world, without any thought of return, then will your work bring you no attachment. Attachment comes only where we expect a return.

If working like slaves results in selfishness and attachment, working as master of our own mind gives rise to the bliss of non-attachment.

We say that we cannot do good without at the same time doing some evil, or do evil without doing some good.

Knowing this, how can we work? There have, therefore, been sects in this world who have in an astoundingly preposterous way preached slow suicide as the only means to get out of the world, because if a man lives, he has to kill poor little animals and plants or do injury to something or some one. So according to them the only way out of the world is to die.

The Jains have preached this doctrine as their highest ideal. This teaching seems to be very logical. But the true solution is found in the Gita. It is the theory of non-attachment, to be attached to nothing while doing our work of life.

Know that you are separated entirely from the world, though you are in the world, and that whatever you may be doing in it, you are not doing that for your own sake. Any action that you do for yourself will bring its effect to bear upon you. If it is a good action, you will have to take the good effect, and if bad, you will have to take the bad effect; but any action that is not done for your own sake, whatever it be, will have no effect on you.

There is to be found a very expressive sentence in our scriptures embodying this idea: "Even if he kill the whole universe (or be himself killed), he is neither the killer nor the killed, when he knows that he is not acting for himself at all."

Therefore Karma-Yoga teaches, "Do not give up the world; live in the world, imbibe its influences as much as you can; but if it be for your own enjoyment's sake, work not at all."

Enjoyment should not be the goal. First kill your self and then take the whole world as yourself; as the old Christians used to say, "The old man must die." This old man is the selfish idea that the whole world is made for our enjoyment.

Foolish parents teach their children to pray, "O Lord, Thou hast created this sun for me and this moon for me," as if the Lord has had nothing else to do than to create everything for these babies.

Do not teach your children such nonsense. Then again, there are people who are foolish in another way: they teach us that all these animals were created for us to kill and eat, and that this universe is for the enjoyment of men. That is all foolishness.

A tiger may say, "Man was created for me," and pray, "O Lord, how wicked are these men who do not come and place themselves before me to be eaten; they are breaking Your law."

If the world is created for us, we are also created for the world. That this world is created for our enjoyment is the most wicked idea that holds us down. This world is not for our sake. Millions pass out of it every year; the world does not feel it; millions of others are supplied in their place. Just as much as the world is for us, so we also are for the world.

To work properly, therefore, you have first to give up the idea of attachment. Secondly, do not mix in the fray, hold yourself as a witness and go on working.

My master used to say, "Look upon your children as a nurse does." The nurse will take your baby and fondle it and play with it and behave towards it as gently as if it were her own child; but as soon as you give her notice to quit, she is ready to start off bag and baggage from the house. Everything in the shape of attachment is forgotten; it will not give the ordinary nurse the least pang to leave your children and take up other children.

Even so are you to be with all that you consider your own. You are the nurse, and if you believe in God, believe that all these things which you consider yours are really His. The greatest weakness often insinuates itself as the greatest good and strength. It is a weakness to think that any one is dependent on me, and that I can do good to another. This belief is the mother of all our attachment, and through this attachment comes all our pain.

We must inform our minds that no one in this universe depends upon us; not one beggar depends on our charity; not one soul on our kindness; not one living thing on our help. All are helped on by nature, and will be so helped even though millions of us were not here. The course of nature will not stop for such as you and me; it is, as already pointed out, only a blessed privilege to you and to me that we are allowed, in the way of helping others, to educate ourselves.

This is a great lesson to learn in life, and when we have learned it fully, we shall never be unhappy; we can go and mix without harm in society anywhere and everywhere. You may have wives and husbands, and regiments of servants, and kingdoms to govern; if only you act on the principle that the world is not for you and does not inevitably need you, they can do you no harm.

This very year some of your friends may have died. Is the world waiting without going on, for them to come again? Is its current stopped? No, it goes on. So drive out of your mind the idea that you have to do something for the world; the world does not require any help from you.

It is sheer nonsense on the part of any man to think that he is born to help the world; it is simply pride, it is selfishness insinuating itself in the form of virtue. When you have trained your mind and your nerves to realise this idea of the world's non-dependence on you or on anybody, there will then be no reaction in the form of pain resulting from work.

When you give something to a man and expect nothing — do not even expect the man to be grateful — his ingratitude will not tell upon you, because you never expected anything, never thought you had any right to anything in the way of a return. You gave him what he deserved; his own Karma got it for him; your Karma made you the carrier thereof.

Why should you be proud of having given away something? You are the porter that carried the money or other kind of gift, and the world deserved it by its own Karma. Where is then the reason for pride in you? There is nothing very great in what you give to the world.

When you have acquired the feeling of non-attachment, there will then be neither good nor evil for you. It is only selfishness that causes the difference between good and evil. It is a very hard thing to understand, but you will come to learn in time that nothing in the universe has power over you until you allow it to exercise such a power. Nothing has power over the Self of man, until the Self becomes a fool and loses independence.

So, by non-attachment, you overcome and deny the power of anything to act upon you. It is very easy to say that nothing has the right to act upon you until you allow it to do so; but what is the true sign of the man who really does not allow anything to work upon him, who is neither happy nor unhappy when acted upon by the external world? The sign is that good or ill fortune causes no change in his mind: in all conditions he continues to remain the same.

In Krishna we find ... two ideas [stand] supreme in his message: The first is the harmony of different ideas; the second is non-attachment. A man can attain to perfection, the highest goal, sitting on a throne, commanding armies, working out big plans for nations. In fact, Krishna's great sermon was preached on the battlefield.

Krishna saw plainly through the vanity of all the mummeries, mockeries, and ceremonials of the old priests; and yet he saw some good in them.

This was the great work of Krishna: to clear our eyes and make us look with broader vision upon humanity in its march upward and onward. His was the first heart that was large enough to see truth in all, his the first lips that uttered beautiful words for each and all.

This Krishna preceded Buddha by some thousand years. ... A great many people do not believe that he ever existed. Some believe that [the worship of Krishna grew out of] the old sun worship. There seem to be several Krishnas: one was mentioned in the Upanishads, another was king, another a general. All have been lumped into one Krishna.

It does not matter much. The fact is, some individual comes who is unique in spirituality. Then all sorts of legends are invented around him. But, all the Bibles and stories which come to be cast upon this one person have to be recast in [the mould of] his character. All the stories of the New Testament have to be modelled upon the accepted life [and] character of Christ. In all of the Indian stories about Buddha the one central note of that whole life is kept up — sacrifice for others.

No one can get anything unless he earns it. This is an eternal law. We may sometimes think it is not so, but in the long run we become convinced of it. A man may struggle all his life for riches; he may cheat thousands, but he finds at last that he did not deserve to become rich, and his life becomes a trouble and a nuisance to him.

We may go on accumulating things for our physical enjoyment, but only what we earn is really ours. A fool may buy all the books in the world, and they will be in his library; but he will be able to read only those that he deserves to; and this deserving is produced by Karma.

Our Karma determines what we deserve and what we can assimilate. We are responsible for what we are; and whatever we wish ourselves to be, we have the power to make ourselves. If what we are now has been the result of our own past actions, it certainly follows that whatever we wish to be in future can be produced by our present actions; so we have to know how to act.

Karma-Yoga explains this secret and teaches where and how to work, how to employ to the greatest advantage the largest part of our energies in the work that is before us. But with this secret we must take into consideration the great objection against work, namely that it causes pain.

All misery and pain come from attachment. I want to do work; I want to do good to a human being; and it is ninety to one that that human being whom I have helped will prove ungrateful and go against me; and the result to me is pain. Such things deter mankind from working; and it spoils a good portion of the work and energy of mankind, this fear of pain and misery.

Karma-Yoga teaches us how to work for work's sake, unattached, without caring who is helped, and what for. The Karma-Yogi works because it is his nature, because he feels that it is good for him to do so, and he has no object beyond that.

His position in this world is that of a giver, and he never cares to receive anything. He knows that he is giving, and does not ask for anything in return and, therefore, he eludes the grasp of misery. The grasp of pain, whenever it comes, is the result of the reaction of "attachment".

I have been asked many times how we can work if we do not have the passion which we generally feel for work. I also thought in that way years ago, but as I am growing older, getting more experience, I find it is not true. The less passion there is, the better we work. The calmer we are, the better for us, and the more the amount of work we can do.

When we let loose our feelings, we waste so much energy, shatter our nerves, disturb our minds, and accomplish very little work. The energy which ought to have gone out as work is spent as mere feeling, which counts for nothing. It is only when the mind is very calm and collected that the whole of its energy is spent in doing good work.

And if you read the lives of the great workers which the world has produced, you will find that they were wonderfully calm men. Nothing, as it were, could throw them off their balance.

That is why the man who becomes angry never does a great amount of work, and the man whom nothing can make angry accomplishes so much. The man who gives way to anger, or hatred, or any other passion, cannot work; he only breaks himself to pieces, and does nothing practical. It is the calm, forgiving, equable, well-balanced mind that does the greatest amount of work.

Do not identify yourself with anything. Hold your mind free. All this that you see, the pains and the miseries, are but the necessary conditions of this world; poverty and wealth and happiness are but momentary; they do not belong to our real nature at all. Our nature is far beyond misery and happiness, beyond every object of the senses, beyond the imagination; and yet we must go on working all the time. "Misery comes through attachment, not through work." As soon as we identify ourselves with the work we do, we feel miserable; but if we do not identify ourselves with it, we do not feel that misery.

If a beautiful picture belonging to another is burnt, a man does not generally become miserable; but when his own picture is burnt, how miserable he feels! Why? Both were beautiful pictures, perhaps copies of the same original; but in one case very much more misery is felt than in the other. It is because in one case he identifies himself with the picture, and not in the other.

This "I and mine" causes the whole misery. With the sense of possession comes selfishness, and selfishness brings on misery. Every act of selfishness or thought of selfishness makes us attached to something, and immediately we are made slaves.

Therefore Karma-Yoga tells us to enjoy the beauty of all the pictures in the world, but not to identify ourselves with any of them. Never say "mine". Whenever we say a thing is "mine", misery will immediately come.

We all understand that desires are wrong, but what is meant by giving up desires? How could life go on? It would be the same suicidal advice, killing the desire and the man too. The solution is this. Not that you should not have property, not that you should not have things which are necessary and things which are even luxuries.

Have all that you want, and more, only know the truth and realise it. Wealth does not belong to anybody. Have no idea of proprietorship, possessorship. You are nobody, nor am I, nor anyone else.

All belongs to the Lord, because the opening verse told us to put the Lord in everything. God is in the wealth that you enjoy. He is in the desire that rises in your mind. He is in the things you buy to satisfy your desire; He is in your beautiful attire, in your beautiful ornaments. This is the line of thought.

All will be metamorphosed as soon as you begin to see things in that light. If you put God in your every movement, in your conversation, in your form, in everything, the whole scene changes, and the world, instead of appearing as one of woe and misery, will become a heaven.

"The kingdom of heaven is within you," says Jesus; so says the Vedanta, and every great teacher. "He that hath eyes to see, let him see, and he that hath ears to hear, let him hear." The Vedanta proves that the truth for which we have been searching all this time is present, and was all the time with us.

In our ignorance, we thought we had lost it, and went about the world crying and weeping, struggling to find the truth, while all along it was dwelling in our own hearts. There alone can we find it.

If we understand the giving up of the world in its old, crude sense, then it would come to this: that we must not work, that we must be idle, sitting like lumps of earth, neither thinking nor doing anything, but must become fatalists, driven about by every circumstance, ordered about by the laws of nature, drifting from place to place.

That would be the result. But that is not what is meant. We must work. Ordinary mankind, driven everywhere by false desire, what do they know of work? The man propelled by his own feelings and his own senses, what does he know about work? He works, who is not propelled by his own desires, by any selfishness whatsoever. He works, who has no ulterior motive in view. He works, who has nothing to gain from work.

Here are the two ways of giving up all attachment. The one is for those who do not believe in God, or in any outside help. They are left to their own devices; they have simply to work with their own will, with the powers of their mind and discrimination, saying, "I must be non-attached".

For those who believe in God there is another way, which is much less difficult. They give up the fruits of work unto the Lord; they work and are never attached to the results.

Whatever they see, feel, hear, or do, is for Him. For whatever good work we may do, let us not claim any praise or benefit. It is the Lord's; give up the fruits unto Him.

Let us stand aside and think that we are only servants obeying the Lord, our Master, and that every impulse for action comes from Him every moment. Whatever thou worshippest, whatever thou perceivest, whatever thou doest, give up all unto Him and be at rest.

Give up all desire and be at peace. Have neither friends nor foes, and live alone. Thus shall we travel having neither friends nor foes, neither pleasure nor pain, neither desire nor jealousy, injuring no creatures, being the cause of injury to no creatures — from mountain to mountain, from village to village, preaching the name of the Lord. Seek no help from high or low, from above or below. Desire nothing — and look upon this vanishing panorama as a witness and let it pass.

Give up all argumentation and other distractions. Is there anything in dry intellectual jargon? It only throws the mind off its balance and disturbs it.

Control the organs of the senses and control the mind. Bear every misery without even knowing that you are miserable. Think of nothing but liberation.

Combine seriousness with childlike naïveté . Live in harmony with all. Give up all idea of egoism, and entertain no sectarian views. Useless wrangling is a great sin.

Give up forever the desire for name and fame and power.

"Give up," says the Veda, "give up." That is the one way, "Give up".न प्रजया धनेन त्यागेनैकेऽमृतत्वमानशुः — "Neither through wealth, nor through progeny, but by giving up alone that immortality is to be reached."

Give up the burden of all deeds to the Lord; give all, both good and bad. Do not keep the good and give only the bad. God helps those who do not help themselves.

Weakness is the one cause of suffering. We become miserable because we are weak. We lie, steal, kill, and commit other crimes, because we are weak. We suffer because we are weak. We die because we are weak. Where there is nothing to weaken us, there is no death nor sorrow. We are miserable through delusion. Give up the delusion, and the whole thing vanishes. It is plain and simple indeed. Through all these philosophical discussions and tremendous mental gymnastics we come to this one religious idea, the simplest in the whole world.

You remember that passage in the sermon of Buddha, how he sent a thought of love towards the south, the north, the east, and the west, above and below, until the whole universe was filled with this lose, so grand, great, and infinite. When you have that feeling, you have true personality. The whole universe is one person; let go the little things. Give up the small for the Infinite, give up small enjoyments for infinite bliss.

Most of the religions understand the fact, but the error into which they all seem to fall is the same; they are carried away by the heart, the feelings. There is evil in the world, give up the world; that is the great teaching, and the only teaching, no doubt.

Give up the world. There cannot be two opinions that to understand the truth everyone of us has to give up error. There cannot be two opinions that everyone of us in order to have good must give up evil; there cannot be two opinions that everyone of us to have life must give up what is death.

And yet, what remains to us, if this theory involves giving up the life of the senses, the life as we know it? And what else do we mean by life? If we give this up, what remains?

In Vedanta alone we find a rational solution of the problem. Here I can only lay before you what the Vedanta seeks to teach, and that is the deification of the world. The Vedanta does not in reality denounce the world. The ideal of renunciation nowhere attains such a height as in the teachings of the Vedanta.

But, at the same time, dry suicidal advice is not intended; it really means deification of the world — giving up the world as we think of it, as we know it, as it appears to us — and to know what it really is. Deify it; it is God alone. We read at the commencement of one of the oldest of the Upanishads, "Whatever exists in this universe is to be covered with the Lord."

We have to cover everything with the Lord Himself, not by a false sort of optimism, not by blinding our eyes to the evil, but by really seeing God in everything. Thus we have to give up the world, and when the world is given up, what remains? God.

Renunciation of the senses and desires is the only way out of this misery. If you want to be spiritual, you must renounce. This is the real test. Give up the world — this nonsense of the senses. There is only one real desire: to know what is true, to be spiritual. No more materialism, no more this egoism, I must become spiritual.

Strong, intense must be the desire. If a man's hands and feet were so tied that he could not move and then if a burning piece of charcoal were placed on his body, he would struggle with all his power to throw it off. When I shall have that sort of extreme desire, that restless struggle, to throw off this burning world, then the time will have come for me to glimpse the Divine Truth.

Give up this little life of yours. What matters it if you die of starvation — you and I and thousands like us — so long as this nation lives? What matters it if this little life goes? Everyone has to die, the saint or the sinner, the rich or the poor. The body never remains for anyone. Arise and awake and be perfectly sincere. Give up your passive attitude, gird your loins and stand up.

The fact being that the Lord is in us, we are He, the eternal subject, the real ego, never to be objectified, and that all this objectifying process is mere waste of time and talent. When the soul becomes aware of this, it gives up objectifying and falls back more and more upon the subjective.

This is the evolution, less and less in the body and more and more in the mind — man the highest form, meaning in Sanskrit manas , thought — the animal that thinks and not the animal that "senses" only. This is what in theology is called "renunciation". The formation of society, the institution of marriage, the love for children, our good works, morality, and ethics are all different forms of renunciation.

All our lives in every society are the subjection of the will, the thirst, the desire. This surrender of the will or the fictitious self — or the desire to jump out of ourselves, as it were — the struggle still to objectify the subject — is the one phenomenon in this world of which all societies and social forms are various modes and stages. Love is the easiest and smoothest way towards the self-surrender or subjection of the will and hatred, the opposite.

Karma-Yoga is purifying the mind by means of work. Now if any work is done, good or bad, it must produce as a result a good or bad effect; no power can stay it, once the cause is present.

Therefore good action producing good Karma, and bad action, bad Karma, the soul will go on in eternal bondage without ever hoping for deliverance. Now Karma belongs only to the body or the mind, never to the Atman (Self); only it can cast a veil before the Atman.

The veil cast by bad Karma is ignorance. Good Karma has the power to strengthen the moral powers. And thus it creates non-attachment; it destroys the tendency towards bad Karma and thereby purifies the mind. But if the work is done with the intention of enjoyment, it then produces only that very enjoyment and does not purify the mind or Chitta.

Therefore all work should be done without any desire to enjoy the fruits thereof. All fear and all desire to enjoy here or hereafter must be banished for ever by the Karma-Yogi. Moreover, this Karma without desire of return will destroy the selfishness, which is the root of all bondage.

The watchword of the Karma-Yogi is "not I, but Thou", and no amount of self-sacrifice is too much for him. But he does this without any desire to go to heaven, or gain name or fame or any other benefit in this world.

Although the explanation and rationale of this unselfish work is only in Jnâna-Yoga, yet the natural divinity of man makes him love all sacrifice simply for the good of others, without any ulterior motive, whatever his creed or opinion. Again, with many the bondage of wealth is very great; and Karma-Yoga is absolutely necessary for them as breaking the crystallisation that has gathered round their love of money.

He is free, he is great, who turns his back upon the world, who has renounced everything, who has controlled his passion, and who thirsts for peace. One may gain political and social independence, but if one is a slave to his passions and desires, one cannot feel the pure joy of real freedom.

It is in the nature of work to be impelled ordinarily by motive and by attachment. In the presence of an ever active Providence who notes even the sparrow's fall, how can man attach any importance to his own work? Will it not be a blasphemy to do so when we know that He is taking care of the minutest things in the world?

We have only to stand in awe and reverence before Him saying, "Thy will be done". The highest men cannot work, for in them there is no attachment. Those whose whole soul is gone into the Self, those whose desires are confined in the Self, who have become ever associated with the Self, for them there is no work.

Such are indeed the highest of mankind; but apart from them every one else has to work. In so working we should never think that we can help on even the least thing in this universe. We cannot. We only help ourselves in this gymnasium of the world. This is the proper attitude of work. If we work in this way, if we always remember that our present opportunity to work thus is a privilege which has been given to us, we shall never be attached to anything.

Millions like you and me think that we are great people in the world; but we all die, and in five minutes the world forgets us. But the life of God is infinite. "Who can live a moment, breathe a moment, if this all-powerful One does not will it?"

He is the ever active Providence. All power is His and within His command. Through His command the winds blow, the sun shines, the earth lives, and death stalks upon the earth. He is the all in all; He is all and in all. We can only worship Him.

Give up all fruits of work; do good for its own sake; then alone will come perfect non-attachment. The bonds of the heart will thus break, and we shall reap perfect freedom. This freedom is indeed the goal of Karma-Yoga.

Attachment

How can this be done? We see that the impression of any action, to which we attach ourselves, remains.

I may meet hundreds of persons during the day, and among them meet also one whom I love; and when I retire at night, I may try to think of all the faces I saw, but only that face comes before the mind — the face which I met perhaps only for one minute, and which I loved; all the others have vanished. My attachment to this particular person caused a deeper impression on my mind than all the other faces.

Physiologically the impressions have all been the same; every one of the faces that I saw pictured itself on the retina, and the brain took the pictures in, and yet there was no similarity of effect upon the mind. Most of the faces, perhaps, were entirely new faces, about which I had never thought before, but that one face of which I got only a glimpse found associations inside. Perhaps I had pictured him in my mind for years, knew hundreds of things about him, and this one new vision of him awakened hundreds of sleeping memories in my mind; and this one impression having been repeated perhaps a hundred times more than those of the different faces together, will produce a great effect on the mind.

Therefore, be "unattached"; let things work; let brain centres work; work incessantly, but let not a ripple conquer the mind. Work as if you were a stranger in this land, a sojourner; work incessantly, but do not bind yourselves; bondage is terrible. This world is not our habitation, it is only one of the many stages through which we are passing.

Remember that great saying of the Sânkhya, "The whole of nature is for the soul, not the soul for nature." The very reason of nature's existence is for the education of the soul; it has no other meaning; it is there because the soul must have knowledge, and through knowledge free itself.

If we remember this always, we shall never be attached to nature; we shall know that nature is a book in which we are to read, and that when we have gained the required knowledge, the book is of no more value to us.

Instead of that, however, we are identifying ourselves with nature; we are thinking that the soul is for nature, that the spirit is for the flesh, and, as the common saying has it, we think that man "lives to eat" and not "eats to live". We are continually making this mistake; we are regarding nature as ourselves and are becoming attached to it; and as soon as this attachment comes, there is the deep impression on the soul, which binds us down and makes us work not from freedom but like slaves.

Learn to help without pitying or feeling that there is any misery. Learn to be the same to enemy and to friend; then when you can do that and no longer have any desire, the goal is attained.

Cut down the banyan tree of desire with the axe of non-attachment, and it will vanish utterly. It is all illusion. "He from whom blight and delusion have fallen, he who has conquered the evils of association, he alone is âzâd (free)."

To love anyone personally is bondage. Love all alike, then all desires fall off.

Time, the "eater of everything", comes, and all has to go. Why try to improve the earth, to paint the butterfly? It all has to go at last. Do not be mere white mice in a treadmill, working always and never accomplishing anything. Every desire is fraught with evil, whether the desire itself be good or evil. It is like a dog jumping for a piece of meat which is ever receding from his reach, and dying a dog's death at last. Do not be like that. Cut off all desire.

By thinking about sense objects, attachment to them is formed. From attachment comes longing, and longing breeds anger.

From anger comes delusion, and from delusion, confused memory. From confused memory comes the ruin of discrimination; and from the ruin of discrimination, a man perishes.

There is then no peace in the heart of a carnal man, nor in him that is addicted to outward things, but in the spiritual and devout man.

The Vedanta philosophy says that this whole universe — mental, physical, moral — is hypnotic. Who is the cause of this hypnotism? You yourself are to blame. This weeping and wailing and knocking your heads into corners [against brick walls, as it were] will not do you the least good.

However, knocking everything [that is hypnotic] on the head [leads to] what is called non-attachment; and clinging to more and more hypnotism is attachment. That is why in all religions you will find they wanted to give up the world, although many of them do not understand it.

There was a poor man who wanted some money; and somehow, he had heard that if he could get hold of a ghost, he might command him to bring money or anything else he liked; so he was very anxious to get hold of a ghost. At last he found a sage with great powers, and besought his help. The sage asked him what he would do with a ghost.

"I want a ghost to work for me; teach me how to get hold of one, sir; I desire it very much," replied the man.

But the sage said, “Don’t disturb yourself, go home.”

The next day the man went again to the sage and began to weep and pray, “Give me a ghost; I must have a ghost, sir, to help me.”

At last the sage was disgusted, and said, “Take this charm, repeat this magic word, and a ghost will come, and whatever you say to him he will do. But beware; they are terrible beings, and must be kept continually busy. If you fail to give him work, he will take your life.”

The man replied, “That is easy; I can give him work for all his life.”

Then he went to a forest, and after long repetition of the magic word, a huge ghost appeared before him, and said, “I am a ghost. I have been conquered by your magic; but you must keep me constantly employed. The moment you fail to give me work I will kill you.”

The man said, “Build me a palace,” and the ghost said, “It is done; the palace is built.” “

Bring me money,” said the man. “Here is your money,” said the ghost.

“Cut this forest down, and build a city in its place.”

"That is done," said the ghost, "anything more?"

Now the man began to be frightened and thought he could give him nothing more to do; he did everything in a trice.

The ghost said, "Give me something to do or I will eat you up."

The poor man could find no further occupation for him, and was frightened. So he ran and ran and at last reached the sage, and said, "Oh, sir, protect my life!"

The sage said, "I will find you a way out. Look at that dog with a curly tail. Draw your sword quickly and cut the tail off and give it to the ghost to straighten out."

The man cut off the dog's tail and gave it to the ghost, saying, "Straighten that out for me."

The ghost took it and slowly and carefully straightened it out, but as soon as he let it go, it instantly curled up again. Once more he laboriously straightened it out, only to find it again curled up as soon as he attempted to let go of it. Again he patiently straightened it out, but as soon as he let it go, it curled up again.

So he went on for days and days, until he was exhausted and said, "I was never in such trouble before in my life. I am an old veteran ghost, but never before was I in such trouble. I will make a compromise with you," he said to the man, "you let me off and I will let you keep all I have given you and will promise not to harm you."

The man was much pleased, and accepted the offer gladly.

This world is like a dog's curly tail, and people have been striving to straighten it out for hundreds of years; but when they let it go, it has curled up again. How could it be otherwise? One must first know how to work without attachment, then one will not be a fanatic.

When we know that this world is like a dog's curly tail and will never get straightened, we shall not become fanatics. If there were no fanaticism in the world, it would make much more progress than it does now.

It is a mistake to think that fanaticism can make for the progress of mankind. On the contrary, it is a retarding element creating hatred and anger, and causing people to fight each other, and making them unsympathetic. We think that whatever we do or possess is the best in the world, and what we do not do or possess is of no value.

So, always remember the instance of the curly tail of the dog whenever you have a tendency to become a fanatic. You need not worry or make yourself sleepless about the world; it will go on without you.

When you have avoided fanaticism, then alone will you work well. It is the level-headed man, the calm man, of good judgment and cool nerves, of great sympathy and love, who does good work and so does good to himself. The fanatic is foolish and has no sympathy; he can never straighten the world, nor himself become pure and perfect.

Let us work without desire for name or fame or rule over others. Let us be free from the triple bonds of lust, greed of gain, and anger. And this truth is with us!

Was Krishna cunning? No, he was not cunning. He tried his best to prevent the war. It was Duryodhana who forced the war. But, when once in the thing, you should not recede — that is the man of duty. Do not run away, it is cowardice. When in the thing, you must do it. You should not budge an inch — of course not for a wrong thing; this war was a righteous war.

The devil comes in many guises — anger in the form of justice — passion in the form of duty. When it first comes, the man knows and then he forgets. Just as your pleaders' conscience; at first they know it is all Badmâshi (roguery), then it is duty to their clients; at last they get hardened.

Leave off your commercial calculating ideas. If you can get rid of your attachment to a single thing, you are on the way to liberation.

Look at Krishna: he was great as a son, as a king, as a father, and all through his life he practiced the marvellous teachings which he preached." "He who in the midst of the greatest activity finds the sweetest peace, and in the midst of the greatest calmness is most active, he has known the secret of life."

Krishna shows the way how to do this — by being non-attached: do everything but do not get identified with anything. You are the soul, the pure, the free, all the time; you are the Witness. Our misery comes, not from work, but by our getting attached to something.

Take for instance, money: money is a great thing to have, earn it, says Krishna; struggle hard to get money, but don't get attached to it. So with children, with wife, husband, relatives, fame, everything; you have no need to shun them, only don't get attached.

There is only one attachment and that belongs to the Lord, and to none other. Work for them, love them, do good to them, sacrifice a hundred lives, if need be, for them, but never be attached. His own life was the exact exemplification of that.

The Practice of Unattachment

Attachment is the source of all our pleasures now. We are attached to our friends, to our relatives; we are attached to our intellectual and spiritual works; we are attached to external objects, so that we get pleasure from them.

What, again, brings misery but this very attachment? We have to detach ourselves to earn joy. If only we had power to detach ourselves at will, there would not be any misery. That man alone will be able to get the best of nature, who, having the power of attaching himself to a thing with all his energy, has also the power to detach himself when he should do so.

The difficulty is that there must be as much power of attachment as that of detachment. There are men who are never attracted by anything. They can never love, they are hard-hearted and apathetic; they escape most of the miseries of life.

But the wall never feels misery, the wall never loves, is never hurt; but it is the wall, after all. Surely it is better to be attached and caught, than to be a wall. Therefore the man who never loves, who is hard and stony, escaping most of the miseries of life, escapes also its joys.

We do not want that. That is weakness, that is death. That soul has not been awakened that never feels weakness, never feels misery. That is a callous state. We do not want that.

At the same time, we not only want this mighty power of love, this mighty power of attachment, the power of throwing our whole soul upon a single object, losing ourselves and letting ourselves be annihilated, as it were, for other souls — which is the power of the gods — but we want to be higher even than the gods.

The perfect man can put his whole soul upon that one point of love, yet he is unattached. How comes this? There is another secret to learn.

The beggar is never happy. The beggar only gets a dole with pity and scorn behind it, at least with the thought behind that the beggar is a low object. He never really enjoys what he gets.

We are all beggars. Whatever we do, we want a return. We are all traders. We are traders in life, we are traders in virtue, we are traders in religion. And alas! we are also traders in love.

If you come to trade, if it is a question of give-and-take, if it is a question of buy-and-sell, abide by the laws of buying and selling. There is a bad time and there is a good time; there is a rise and a fall in prices: always you expect the blow to come. It is like looking at the mirrors Your face is reflected: you make a grimace — there is one in the mirror; if you laugh, the mirror laughs. This is buying and selling, giving and taking.

We get caught. How? Not by what we give, but by what we expect. We get misery in return for our love; not from the fact that we love, but from the fact that we want love in return. There is no misery where there is no want. Desire, want, is the father of all misery. Desires are bound by the laws of success and failure. Desires must bring misery.

The great secret of true success, of true happiness, then, is this: the man who asks for no return, the perfectly unselfish man, is the most successful. It seems to be a paradox. Do we not know that every man who is unselfish in life gets cheated, gets hurt? Apparently, yes. "Christ was unselfish, and yet he was crucified." True, but we know that his unselfishness is the reason, the cause of a great victory — the crowning of millions upon millions of lives with the blessings of true success.

Ask nothing; want nothing in return. Give what you have to give; it will come back to you — but do not think of that now, it will come back multiplied a thousandfold — but the attention must not be on that. Yet have the power to give: give, and there it ends. Learn that the whole of life is giving, that nature will force you to give.

So, give willingly. Sooner or later you will have to give up. You come into life to accumulate. With clenched hands, you want to take. But nature puts a hand on your throat and makes your hands open. Whether you will it or not, you have to give.

The moment you say, "I will not", the blow comes; you are hurt. None is there but will be compelled, in the long run, to give up everything.

And the more one struggles against this law, the more miserable one feels. It is because we dare not give, because we are not resigned enough to accede to this grand demand of nature, that we are miserable.

The forest is gone, but we get heat in return. The sun is taking up water from the ocean, to return it in showers. You are a machine for taking and giving: you take, in order to give.

Ask, therefore, nothing in return; but the more you give, the more will come to you. The quicker you can empty the air out of this room, the quicker it will be filled up by the external air; and if you close all the doors and every aperture, that which is within will remain, but that which is outside will never come in, and that which is within will stagnate, degenerate, and become poisoned.

A river is continually emptying itself into the ocean and is continually filling up again. Bar not the exit into the ocean. The moment you do that, death seizes you.

Be, therefore, not a beggar; be unattached. This is the most terrible task of life! You do not calculate the dangers on the path. Even by intellectually recognising the difficulties, we really do not know them until we feel them.

From a distance we may get a general view of a park: well, what of that? We feel and really know it when we are in it. Even if our every attempt is a failure, and we bleed and are torn asunder, yet, through all this, we have to preserve our heart — we must assert our Godhead in the midst of all these difficulties.

Nature wants us to react, to return blow for blow, cheating for cheating, lie for lie, to hit back with all our might. Then it requires a superdivine power not to hit back, to keep control, to be unattached.

Every day we renew our determination to be unattached. We cast our eyes back and look at the past objects of our love and attachment, and feel how every one of them made us miserable. We went down into the depths of despondency because of our "love"! We found ourselves mere slaves in the hands of others, we were dragged down and down!

And we make a fresh determination: "Henceforth, I will be master of myself; henceforth, I will have control over myself." But the time comes, and the same story once more! Again the soul is caught and cannot get out. The bird is in a net, struggling and fluttering. This is our life.

I know the difficulties. Tremendous they are, and ninety per cent of us become discouraged and lose heart, and in our turn, often become pessimists and cease to believe in sincerity, love, and all that is grand and noble.

So, we find men who in the freshness of their lives have been forgiving, kind, simple, and guileless, become in old age lying masks of men. Their minds are a mass of intricacy. There may be a good deal of external policy, possibly. They are not hot-headed, they do not speak, but it would be better for them to do so; their hearts are dead and, therefore, they do not speak.

They do not curse, not become angry; but it would be better for them to be able to be angry, a thousand times better, to be able to curse. They cannot. There is death in the heart, for cold hands have seized upon it, and it can no more act, even to utter a curse, even to use a harsh word.

All this we have to avoid: therefore I say, we require superdivine power. Superhuman power is not strong enough. Superdivine strength is the only way, the one way out. By it alone we can pass through all these intricacies, through these showers of miseries, unscathed. We may be cut to pieces, torn asunder, yet our hearts must grow nobler and nobler all the time.

It is very difficult, but we can overcome the difficulty by constant practice. We must learn that nothing can happen to us, unless we make ourselves susceptible to it. I have just said, no disease can come to me until the body is ready; it does not depend alone on the germs, but upon a certain predisposition which is already in the body. We get only that for which we are fitted.

Let us give up our pride and understand this, that never is misery undeserved. There never has been a blow undeserved: there never has been an evil for which I did not pave the way with my own hands. We ought to know that. Analyse yourselves and you will find that every blow you have received, came to you because you prepared yourselves for it. You did half, and the external world did the other half: that is how the blow came. That will sober us down.

At the same time, from this very analysis will come a note of hope, and the note of hope is: "I have no control of the external world, but that which is in me and nearer unto me, my own world, is in my control. If the two together are required to make a failure, if the two together are necessary to give me a blow, I will not contribute the one which is in my keeping; and how then can the blow come? If I get real control of myself, the blow will never come."

By non-attachment and practice, meditation is perfected.

"I cannot tell anything about Thee except that Thou art my love. Thou art beautiful, Oh, Thou art beautiful! Thou art beauty itself." What is after all really required of us in this Yoga is that our thirst after the beautiful should be directed to God. What is the beauty in the human face, in the sky, in the stars, and in the moon? It is only the partial apprehension of the real all-embracing Divine Beauty. "He shining, everything shines. It is through His light that all things shine."

Take this high position of Bhakti which makes you forget at once all your little personalities. Take yourself away from all the world's little selfish clingings. Do not look upon humanity as the centre of all your human and higher interests. Stand as a witness, as a student, and observe the phenomena of nature.

Have the feeling of personal non-attachment with regard to man, and see how this mighty feeling of love is working itself out in the world. Sometimes a little friction is produced, but that is only in the course of the struggle to attain the higher real love. Sometimes there is a little fight or a little fall; but it is all only by the way. Stand aside, and freely let these frictions come. You feel the frictions only when you are in the current of the world, but when you are outside of it simply as a witness and as a student, you will be able to see that there are millions and millions of channels in which God is manifesting Himself as Love.

The Bhakti-Yogi knows the meaning of life's struggles; he understands it. He has passed through a long series of these struggles and knows what they mean and earnestly desires to be free from the friction thereof; he wants to avoid the clash and go direct to the centre of all attraction, the great Hari.

This is the renunciation of the Bhakta. This mighty attraction in the direction of God makes all other attractions vanish for him. This mighty infinite love of God which enters his heart leaves no place for any other love to live there. How can it be otherwise? Bhakti fills his heart with the divine waters of the ocean of love, which is God Himself; there is no place there for little loves. That is to say, the Bhakta's renunciation is that Vairâgya or non-attachment for all things that are not God which results from Anurâga or great attachment to God.

Whenever we say a thing is "mine", misery will immediately come. Do not even say "my child" in your mind. Possess the child, but do not say "mine". If you do, then will come the misery.

Do not say "my house," do not say "my body". The whole difficulty is there. The body is neither yours, nor mine, nor anybody's. These bodies are coming and going by the laws of nature, but we are free, standing as witness.

This body is no more free than a picture or a wall. Why should we be attached so much to a body? If somebody paints a picture, he does it and passes on. Do not project that tentacle of selfishness, "I must possess it". As soon as that is projected, misery will begin.

So Karma-Yoga says, first destroy the tendency to project this tentacle of selfishness, and when you have the power of checking it, hold it in and do not allow the mind to get into the ways of selfishness. Then you may go out into the world and work as much as you can. Mix everywhere, go where you please; you will never be contaminated with evil. There is the lotus leaf in the water; the water cannot touch and adhere to it; so will you be in the world. This is called "Vairâgya", dispassion or non-attachment.

I believe I have told you that without non-attachment there cannot be any kind of Yoga. Non-attachment is the basis of all the Yogas. The man who gives up living in houses, wearing fine clothes, and eating good food, and goes into the desert, may be a most attached person. His only possession, his own body, may become everything to him; and as he lives he will be simply struggling for the sake of his body.

Non-attachment does not mean anything that we may do in relation to our external body, it is all in the mind. The binding link of "I and mine" is in the mind. If we have not this link with the body and with the things of the senses, we are non-attached, wherever and whatever we may be. A man may be on a throne and perfectly non-attached; another man may be in rags and still very much attached.

First, we have to attain this state of non-attachment and then to work incessantly. Karma-Yoga gives us the method that will help us in giving up all attachment, though it is indeed very hard.

The body is our enemy, and yet is our friend. Which of you can bear the sight of misery? And which of you cannot do so when you see it only as a painting? Because it is unreal, we do not identify ourselves with it, eve know it is only a painting; it cannot bless us, it cannot hurt us.

The most terrible misery painted upon a price of canvas, we may even enjoy; we praise the technique of the artist, we wonder at his marvellous genius, even though the scene he paints is most horrible. That is the secret; that non-attachment. Be the Witness.

Since I was a child I have heard about Krishna's life. I take it for granted there must have been a man called Krishna, and his Gita shows he has [left] a wonderful book.

I told you, you can understand the character of a man by analysing the fables about him. The fables have the nature [of decorations]. You must find they are all polished and manipulated to fit into the character.

For instance, take Buddha. The central idea [is] sacrifice. There are thousands of folklore, but in every case the sacrifice must have been kept up.

There are thousands of stories about Lincoln, about some characteristic of that great man. You take all the fables and find the general idea and [know] that that was the central character of the man.

You find in Krishna that non-attachment is the central idea. He does not need anything. He does not want anything. He works for work's sake. "Work for work's sake. Worship for worship's sake. Do good because it is good to do good. Ask no more."

That must have been the character of the man. Otherwise these fables could not be brought down to the one idea of non-attachment.

The purer the body and mind, the quicker the desired result will be obtained. You must be perfectly pure. Do not think of evil things, such thoughts will surely drag you down.

If you are perfectly pure and practice faithfully, your mind can finally be made a searchlight of infinite power. There is no limit to its scope.

But there must be constant practice and non-attachment to the world. When a man reaches the superconscious state, all feeling of body melts away. Then alone does he become free and immortal.

Unselfishness

There is to be found in every religion the manifestation of this struggle towards freedom. It is the groundwork of all morality, of unselfishness, which means getting rid of the idea that men are the same as their little body. When we see a man doing good work, helping others, it means that he cannot be confined within the limited circle of "me and mine". There is no limit to this getting out of selfishness. All the great systems of ethics preach absolute unselfishness as the goal. Supposing this absolute unselfishness can be reached by a man, what becomes of him? He is no more the little Mr. So-and-so; he has acquired infinite expansion. The little personality which he had before is now lost to him for ever; he has become infinite, and the attainment of this infinite expansion is indeed the goal of all religions and of all moral and philosophical teachings. The personalist, when he hears this idea philosophically put, gets frightened. At the same time, if he preaches morality, he after all teaches the very same idea himself. He puts no limit to the unselfishness of man. Suppose a man becomes perfectly unselfish under the personalistic system, how are we to distinguish him from the perfected ones in other system? He has become one with the universe and to become that is the goal of all; only the poor personalist has not the courage to follow out his own reasoning to its right conclusion. Karma-Yoga is the attaining through unselfish work of that freedom which is the goal of all human nature. Every selfish action, therefore, retards our reaching the goal, and every unselfish action takes us towards the goal; that is why the only definition that can be given of morality is this: That which is selfish is immoral, and that which is unselfish is moral .

Above all, to do good, perfect unselfishness is absolutely necessary.

With every breath, every impulse of our heart asks us to be selfish. At the same time, there is some power beyond us which says that it is unselfishness alone which is good.

It is unswerving love and perfect unselfishness that conquer everything.

Of one thing I am sure — that whoever wants to help his fellow beings through genuine love and unselfishness will work wonders.

Can any man deny that love, this “not I”, this renunciation is the only positive power in the universe? That other is only the misguided employment of the power of love; the power of love brings competition, the real genesis of competition is in love. The real genesis of evil is in unselfishness. The creator of evil is good, and the end is also good. It is only misdirection of the power of good. A man who murders another is, perhaps, moved to do so by the love of his own child. His love has become limited to that one little baby, to the exclusion of the millions of other human beings in the universe. Yet, limited or unlimited, it is the same love.

The motive power of the whole universe, in what ever way it manifests itself, is this one wonderful thing, unselfishness, renunciation, love, the real, the only living force in existence.

There is a false sentiment which goes the extreme of unselfishness, only to injure others by its submission to every evil. We have no right to make others selfish by our unselfishness; have we?

Self-Abnegation

You will find various classes of men in this world. There are the God-men, whose self-abnegation is complete, and who do only good to others even at the sacrifice of their own lives. These are the highest of men. If there are a hundred of such in any country, that country need never despair.

But they are unfortunately too few. Then there are the good men who do good to others so long as it does not injure themselves. And there is a third class who, to do good to themselves, injure others.

It is said by a Sanskrit poet that there is a fourth unnamable class of people who injure others merely for injury's sake. Just as there are at one pole of existence the highest good men, who do good for the sake of doing good, so, at the other pole, there are others who injure others just for the sake of the injury. They do not gain anything thereby, but it is their nature to do evil.

Here are two Sanskrit words. The one is Pravritti, which means revolving towards, and the other is Nivritti, which means revolving away. The "revolving towards" is what we call the world, the "I and mine"; it includes all those things which are always enriching that "me" by wealth and money and power, and name and fame, and which are of a grasping nature, always tending to accumulate everything in one centre, that centre being "myself".

That is the Pravritti, the natural tendency of every human being; taking everything from everywhere and heaping it around one centre, that centre being man's own sweet self. When this tendency begins to break, when it is Nivritti or "going away from," then begin morality and religion. Both Pravritti and Nivritti are of the nature of work: the former is evil work, and the latter is good work.

This Nivritti is the fundamental basis of all morality and all religion, and the very perfection of it is entire self-abnegation, readiness to sacrifice mind and body and everything for another being. When a man has reached that state, he has attained to the perfection of Karma-Yoga.

It is not at all any question of creed, or doctrine — even men who are very much opposed to all religious ideas, when they see one of these acts of complete self-sacrifice, feel that they must revere it.

Have you not seen even a most bigoted Christian, when he reads Edwin Arnold's Light of Asia, stand in reverence of Buddha, who Preached no God, preached nothing but self-sacrifice?

The only thing is that the bigot does not know that his own end and aim in life is exactly the same as that of those from whom he differs. The worshipper, by keeping constantly before him the idea of God and a surrounding of good, comes to the same point at last and says, "Thy will be done," and keeps nothing to himself. That is self-abnegation.

The philosopher, with his knowledge, sees that the seeming self is a delusion and easily gives it up. It is self-abnegation. So Karma, Bhakti, and Jnana all meet here; and this is what was meant by all the great preachers of ancient times, when they taught that God is not the world.

There is one thing which is the world and another which is God; and this distinction is very true. What they mean by world is selfishness. Unselfishness is God. One may live on a throne, in a golden palace, and be perfectly unselfish; and then he is in God. Another may live in a hut and wear rags, and have nothing in the world; yet, if he is selfish, he is intensely merged in the world.

Every act of charity, every thought of sympathy, every action of help, every good deed, is taking so much of self-importance away from our little selves and making us think of ourselves as the lowest and the least, and, therefore, it is all good. Here we find that Jnâna, Bhakti, and Karma — all come to one point.

The highest ideal is eternal and entire self-abnegation, where there is no "I," but all is "Thou"; and whether he is conscious or unconscious of it, Karma-Yoga leads man to that end. A religious preacher may become horrified at the idea of an Impersonal God; he may insist on a Personal God and wish to keep up his own identity and individuality, whatever he may mean by that.

But his ideas of ethics, if they are really good, cannot but be based on the highest self-abnegation. It is the basis of all morality; you may extend it to men, or animals, or angels, it is the one basic idea, the one fundamental principle running through all ethical systems.

The more a man throws himself away, the more God comes in, hence self abnegation, which is the secret of all religion and morality. Too many people bring down their ideals. They want a comfortable religion, but there is none such. It is all self-surrender and upward striving.

What is perfect self-abnegation? It means the abnegation of this apparent self, the abnegation of all selfishness. This idea of "me and mine" — Ahamkâra and Mamatâ — is the result of past Superstition, and the more this present self passes away, the more the real Self becomes manifest.

This is true self-abnegation, the centre, the basis, the gist of all moral teaching; and whether man knows it or not the whole world is slowly going towards it, practicing it more or less. Only, the vast majority of mankind are doing it unconsciously. Let them do it consciously. Let then make the sacrifice, knowing that this "me and mine" is not the real Self, but only a limitation.

But one glimpse Of that infinite reality which is behind — but one spark of that infinite fire that is the All — represents the present man; the Infinite is his true nature.

If we are genuine Karma-Yogis and wish to train ourselves to that attainment of this state, wherever we may begin we are sure to end in perfect self-abnegation; and as soon as this seeming self has gone, the whole world, which at first appears to us to be filled with evil, will appear to be heaven itself and full of blessedness. Its very atmosphere will be blessed; every human face there will be god. Such is the end and aim of Karma-Yoga, and such is its perfection in practical life.

The mission of the Institute of Thought and Philosophy is to preserve and propagate the teachings of Swami Vivekananda. This great Indian spiritual leader is known for introducing the West to Hinduism. Drawing from his vast literary legacy, we provide valuable insights and practical guidance for modern living.

Have any query or feedback? Please reach out to us at

ITPPress123@gmail.com